GETTING MORE
OUT OF LIFE

Copies of this book may be ordered from the distributor

Star Publishing Company, Inc.
609 North Railroad Avenue
Boynton Beach, Florida 33435

Price: $7.95 a copy, plus $1.50 postage and handling
Five copies: $32.00 (20% discount),
plus $2.50 postage and handling

Cover graphics by Kim Starkey

Printed and bound in the United States of America

For Isabel
who by getting more out of her life
has given so much more to my life
With love and gratitude

Contents

A Word to the Reader

Some people who pick up this little book will be men and women who have known an abundance of satisfaction and happiness in life. Others may have found the going rougher, the rewards fewer, the sunshine a shade less bright. Still others, and I do hope their ranks are few, may have known enough of discouragement, disappointment and defeat that clouds too often shadow their skies.

And yet I suppose that all of us, from the most sanguine to the least hopeful, would like, in the words of our book title, to get at least a little more out of life than we are presently getting. Naturally. There is something elemental in our nature that drives us to seek ever more substance, meaning, value in the human experience. Getting more out of life, and giving more to life, is what the game is all about.

Having said as much, however, let me hasten to add that this varied volume makes no grandiose claims. It purports to be neither a guidebook to happiness, nor a how-to-achieve-success manual, nor a ready-mix of wisdom and revelation. It is simply a sharing, by me with you, of an assortment of ideas, insights, experiences and lessons I have had or learned as I have traveled our common road.

For more than forty years now on the lecture platform, at the radio microphone, through my writing and in the ministry, increasingly I have discovered how much people appreciate such a sharing. Like unexpected flowers along the way, I have often found small examples or illuminations that have helped me face the daily challenge with a little more courage and confidence, and I have tried to share these with my audiences and readers. And that is what I hope to do here.

Some years ago as part of a lecture series at the Twentieth Century Club of Pittsburgh, I gave a more-personal-than-usual address. In it I talked about a parcel of lessons from life I have learned that have had special meaning and value for me. Afterward, one of the members of the audience said, "Dr. Argow, I liked what you had to say and the way you said it, and I have a suggestion to make: Why don't you write a book along the same lines you were following today?"

Now I have already made my disclaimer: I have no illusions about my status as wise man or spiritual cheerleader. Yet the more I thought about that woman's proposal — others had made it too — the more it appealed to me. I have been slow in implementing it, but increasingly I have felt a hankering for such a book, or books. Heaven knows, the world these days needs as much assurance, fortitude and commitment to ideal ends as it can muster. In any event, these seventy-seven random pieces are my response to a thoughtful, appreciated suggestion.

It should scarcely be necessary to add that I do not envision anybody sitting down and reading this book in one or two sessions. It is the sort of thing a person dips into as the mood or the need directs. Pick it up and read it for fun and, let us piously hope, profit. Take it along on a vacation. Lend it to or, preferably, buy it for a friend. In the midst of a busy day, open it for a few minutes for the pause that refreshes (either classic or without sugar).

But most of all, gentle reader, I like to think of you in the interval before bedtime. You have opened the book, leafed through it for a few minutes and found a meaning or a message that somehow helps bring the day to a tranquil close.

And then, just before you turn out the light, you read one more page. It is a passage that, in the way words can sometimes do, enhances your hope for the day that lies ahead, and your confidence, and your eagerness to get . . . still more out of life.

Waldemar Argow
Maple Juice Cove
Cushing, Maine
July 1987

"Christina's World"

The most renowned and the most popularly-acclaimed artist in America today is Andrew Wyeth. Of the many superb paintings Wyeth has produced, the best known is one he did in 1948 called "Christina's World." Indeed, it is probably the most famous painting given us by an American artist in this century.

In the right background of the picture stands a bleak, unpainted, weatherbeaten Maine farmhouse. Then there is a great field of dry grass that covers most of the canvas. And down in the lower left-hand corner is a young woman in a pink dress crawling toward the house. The woman is Christina Olson, who had been increasingly crippled by a birth defect or injury, and the old farmhouse was her family home. One day Wyeth, whose own summer home is only a few miles away, saw Miss Olson crawling through the grass toward her house, and he was so moved by the scene and various meanings it symbolized or suggested that he painted this tempera.

The reason I know so much about the picture is that there is a sense in which my wife and I "own" it. Oh, not the Wyeth canvas, but the original scene. The Olson farm stands on a hill overlooking Maple Juice Cove to the west and a splendid sweep of St. George River estuary, Muscongus Bay islands and Atlantic Ocean to the south. Half a mile across the waters of Maple Juice Cove is the summer home my wife Isabel and I have lived in and loved for almost 25 years. When we look to the east, there they are, the Olson farm and the field of dry grass. We see them from much the same vantage point from which Wyeth painted his haunting picture. Little has changed in more than 35 years.

Terribly handicapped though she was, alone much of the time, still Miss Olson continued to live in the old house until the day of her death in 1968. In order to be by her sea and her spruce wood and her sea gulls crying, and to preserve her independence — her fierce, rugged, precious independence — she scorned the very thought of nursing homes and institutions. Her world may have been tiny and unkempt, bitterly cold in winter and lonely as death, but it had an integrity about it that made it, in its own way, great.

At every hour of the day and night I have looked across our tidal flats and seen . . . Christina's world. I have seen it at sunset, the house, strange, spare, almost forbidding in the dying light. And I have seen it in the dark of night, still dimly visible, still exuding an air of lowering mystery. It reminds me of "The Fall of the House of Usher" or the New England tragedies of Eugene O'Neill. And always the sight moves me profoundly for I find it a symbol of a courage that scorned adversity and was determined to get as much as it possibly could out of life, a courage as rugged and persevering as the granite ledges around it.

Only Andrew Wyeth could have done it justice. The man paints in a seemingly naturalistic or realistic way, yet he has called himself an "abstractionist artist." He means, one supposes, that there are values, subtleties, nuances in his work that are simply suggested, felt, implied rather than represented. So many of his canvases are suffused with a lorn, eerie quality — curtains blowing in a wind from the sea, a chair standing forsaken in a field, a boat abandoned a few feet above high tide line. One has a sense of ghosts hovering, or spirits just departed. Christina's is a haunted house in an empty silence, yet like the chair and the boat it is nonetheless real for all that. In the elusive, affecting way he has, Andrew Wyeth has projected a reality deeper and more telling than mere surface appearance.

During my lifetime I have cruised and flown around the world and traveled pretty much all over it. But I have learned one of its dearest lessons right in my own backyard and the lesson is this: that no matter how small one's own personal world may be, it can still be a big world, a great world, if one will face it with dignity, integrity and courage. It is a lesson I have learned from, and that I remember every time I look across the waters of Maple Juice Cove to . . . Christina's world.

Life is a Laughing Matter

"Humor is the greatest quality a human being can have." That's what Mark Van Doren, a distinguished American poet and scholar, said on the occasion of his 75th birthday in 1969. It seems safe to assume he was doing what poets frequently do and that was indulge in a little poetic license. Another name for it in this instance might have been exaggeration.

What Van Doren was probably suggesting in the devious way poets have is that humor is a far more important — and serious — component of human life than we realize. Humor is nothing to laugh at. It holds our lives in balance, gives us perspective, keeps us in touch with reality. Three thousand years ago in **The Iliad** Homer said, "Laughter shakes the skies." It also helps stabilize the earth.

No people have had a more robust and rollicking sense of humor than we Americans. Think of Oliver Wendell Holmes, Abe Lincoln, Mark Twain, Bret Harte, Josh Billings, Finley Peter Dunne, Artemis Ward, Will Rogers, Robert Benchley and James Thurber. Two years before he died, Thurber said about humor, "I like to think of it as one of our greatest and earliest natural resources."

In the light of our happy history of humor it is all the more dolorous to realize how dry the wells have lately been running. We seem to feel that in a world like ours joking and jesting are out of place. There is a time to laugh and a time to cry and our timing is bad. Oh, we have plenty of stand-up comics, TV comedies and the like, but they are feeble substitutes for that bucolic and ribald, but also shrewd and knowing humor that was "one of our greatest . . . natural resources."

Some commentators think that Vietnam, Watergate, the nuclear threat, our dubious American future are responsible. And they may be right. But we are wrong if we feel that laughter is in poor taste these days, as with clowns at a funeral. The blessed sanity of humor: there is nothing quite like it. We must take the world seriously, of course — but not too seriously. The trouble with deadly seriousness is that it is precisely that — deadly.

This is why through the centuries comedy has ranked with tragedy as one of the most splendid creations of the human spirit. If it is imperative that we see the Promethean creature man can be and the heights and depths to which he can go, it is equally important that we see and sympathize with the foolish but lovable fellow he usually is and the preposterous capacity he has for stumbling and bumbling and still surviving. Comedy can teach us quite as much as tragedy. We cherish it, not only because it is funny, but also because it is true.

Indeed, the reason we today do not hold comedy in specially high regard is that we tend to think of it in terms of mere funniness. We do not appreciate Henry Ward Beecher's observation that "A man without a sense of humor is like a wagon without springs; he is jolted by every pebble in the road." That's what happens to humorless people. Because they have no sense of proportion or perspective, no built-in shock absorbers to help cushion the bounce, they are jolted by every pothole in the pavement.

And we all sometimes experience those jolts. When you and I are wound up too tightly, when we are unduly worried or frightened or angry, our vision is knocked askew. There is a distortion of perspective. But if we can find the grace and good sense to laugh at ourselves, the world tilts back toward level again and we see life as it actually is, a pretty fine and fascinating adventure, on the whole.

There is also this to be said about the therapeutic value of humor. Humor is one thing arrogance, ostentation, conceit, vanity simply cannot stand up against. It deflates and diminishes them as nothing else can. Have you ever known a really prejudiced man or woman with a healthy sense of humor? Or a mean, selfish, vindictive person who could laugh at himself? I doubt it. Tolerance, goodwill, comradeship, common sense, understanding, reason, compassion have no better friend than humor. Who can hate the person he laughs with? Who can disparage and despise himself when he is secretly amused and entertained by himself?

Mark Van Doren may have exaggerated a bit, but that's all right, he was a poet; and, besides, he was on the right track. If you and I want to get more from life, as who doesn't?, we had better take a leaf out of Van Doren's book. And also one out of an obscure eighteenth century versifier's. Matthew Green had honed his humor to a pinpoint and, wasting no time about the matter, said shortly, "Laugh and be well."

Life is What You Make It

Probably the most popular character in all mythology is the Good Fairy. The Good Fairy grants wishes. Like your wacky aunt from Wichita, she pops up unexpectedly. She visits you to grant one, and only one, wish which is guaranteed to come true. (Like Santa Claus, the Good Fairy is somebody I don't really believe in — but I shyly have to confess I'd like to.)

Putting me and my dreary skepticism aside for the moment, however, let's suppose the Good Fairy wondrously does materialize and calls on you and your neighbors. One wish, says she, and it must be a personal wish. Even I can't do anything about the politicians and their witless wars, foreign (a word that means strange) policies and nuclear threats. So, what'll you have?

For the Bennetts next door, it's a winter hideaway in the Tucson Mountains. For young Susie Sanders across the street, it's the teenager's dream of Hollywood success. For another neighbor, becoming president of his company. For still another, retirement to sun country. And for you? How about a nice one-man-or-woman business of your own?

A gaggle of years flies by and time confirms that G.F. was as good as her word; the dreams have come to pass — Hollywood success, sun country, money in the bank, the whole glittering batch. And what does it all mean? What has it brought or meant to you and your friends? Ay, there's the rub. To a disconcerting and unexpected extent, life isn't all that much different.

Success, yes; prestige, bigger income, more sunshine, golf and outings with the boys or girls. But if happiness could be measured in a qualitative way, would you say that you and your friends are appreciably happier now than you were then, back in the old neighborhood?

The baffling answer may well be no. It was Oscar Wilde who said, "In this world there are only two tragedies. One is not getting what one wants, and the other is getting it." At first glance, Wilde's proposition doesn't seem to make much sense. Why in the world wouldn't we be happier and more content with the fulfillment of our dreams?

The answer, the puzzling but enormously important answer, is that happiness and satisfaction in life essentially depend on taking the raw materials around us at any given time and finding our gratification and fulfillment through them. And whether it's on East Factory Street in Buffalo or South Ocean Boulevard in Palm Beach, whether it's with an average man's means or a rich man's money, the difference isn't all that great. Here's how Lincoln summed it up, "Most people are about as happy as they make up their minds to be." That was Lincoln's way of saying that life is what you make it.

Socrates going barefoot in Athens was, we may assume, a happier man than Aristotle Onassis with all his multi-millions. Rich big-shots are probably no more content than poor little-shots, though they may be more comfortable.

Such sentiments as these are not intended to reflect some sort of anti-materialistic, poor-is-better philosophy. Nobody in his right mind would exchange the standard of living we enjoy in the United States for that of India. Comfort and well-being; the sensibly chosen good things that money can buy; the doors it can open; the travel opportunities it affords; the means it provides to aid those good causes we believe in; the horizons it can help broaden — all of these are blessings for which those of us privileged to have should never cease giving thanks.

The great verity involved here, however, is this: that material possession and worldly acclaim are no guarantee whatsoever of happiness. In fact, unwisely handled, as they frequently are, they bring something like the opposite of happiness. In a society as generally prosperous and fortunate as ours, even the more judicious among us sometimes have trouble accepting what I have called the Great Verity. But, like Margaret Thatcher and her universe, "By God, we'd better accept it!"

If you and I are going to know much satisfaction and serenity in life, we must take what we have, here, now, this day, and use and enjoy and find meaning in it. This person I love, these friends, that sunset, this book or music, this particular skill I have developed and that I delight in using, these worldly goods I can share with others: if there is any one secret of happiness, we may find it here.

I wish Confucius or Socrates or the Oracle at Delphi had spoken these words; they would then seem more consequential (and I guess, in a way, they did speak them). In any event, whoever said it and however he or she said it, the ineluctable fact remains that — life is what you make it.

On Paying the Price

Among the world's major living religions, Hinduism is considered to be the oldest; it has roots straggling back at least five millenia. So diverse are its beliefs and practices that "Hinduism" is really a kind of umbrella term. Yet it does have certain unifying elements, and one is the doctrine of karma with its concomitant belief in reincarnation. This is the conviction that when we die not ony are we born again, but in our next existence we enjoy the fruits, or pay for the misdeeds, of our present life. Moreoever, this process of birth and rebirth, of reward and punishment, goes on, for most souls, interminably. Thus is good compensated and evil chastised. Thus, inescapably, inexorably, we pay the price.

The doctrine of karma and reincarnation really has no counterpart in the Judaeo-Christian tradition — and occasionally Jews and Christians mournfully confess that they wish it had. Life would seem so much fairer if we could be assured of a divine mechanism, some sort of **deus ex machina,** by which the good guys are always rewarded and the bad guys get what they jolly well deserve.

Regrettably, though, the world doesn't seem to operate as it properly should. Think of all the crooks and con men, the gamblers and gangsters who have amassed awesome tax-free fortunes and have never seen the inside of a hoosegow. Think of Percival Vanderocks who inherited 25 million green ones and has never done a real day's work in his life. In fact, the world is full of people who haven't worked as hard or done as much as we have, and yet look at them sitting in their air-conditioned castles on their ill-begotten gains. It simply isn't fair, we say. Somehow, some way, they ought to have to pay the price.

What we must understand is that there are a good many laws and principles in this world that apply in general, on the whole, over the long haul; they do not inevitably pertain in every instance as the law of gravitation does (at least by Newtonian definition). There are no statutory laws that are always fair, equitable, just. Even the wisest of judges sometimes errs and the most competent of juries makes deadly mistakes. About the best that can be said is that generally speaking, for the most part, our laws, judges and juries are as fair and equitable as we can reasonably expect.

That's the way it is with the "paying the price" principle we are talking about here. Despite the many exceptions any of us can think of, it is still fundamentally true that on the whole we get what we deserve and what we pay for in this world. If it were not so, do you suppose civilized society could have come into being and have continued to exist as it has? If it were not so, what would be the point of goodness, honesty, principle, morality, faith? We trust them because we know that, in the long run, they do prevail, that they are pragmatically justified by the common experience of the human race.

It is, of course, that "on the whole" that bothers us. We are inclined to think of the exceptions. What about this man whose life has been ruined by the double-dealing and deceit of his associates? What about that much-beloved mother of five tragically killed in a senseless accident? Cruel, unfair, merciless? The wrathful answer has to be yes.

Part of our trouble here is that most of us have a tendency to think in terms of absolutes. We say that crime doesn't pay. Which, of course, is untrue; obviously, sometimes it does. We say that virtue triumphs and love conquers all; that the wicked are punished and the good receive their just reward. Right — most of the time, enough of the time to validate them and to make this principle worth living, and dying, for. But not always inevitably true.

So? So we have to learn to live with some degree of ambiguity. We have to accept the fact that while the odds stoutly favor the good, the just, the true, there is no immutable decree written into the nature of the universe which promises that the good guys will **always** prevail.

Sometimes it's difficult to understand, and to make any kind of sensible computation, and to see the truth for its few exceptions. But, count on it — on the whole, over the long haul, whether of a single life or of human history, the enormously heartening and sustaining evidence is that we do pay the price and we do get what we pay for.

Burt Reynolds' Ducks

Ocean Parks is one of the more attractive and spacious condominium developments along the north Palm Beaches on the east coast of Florida. It faces the ocean to the east with the Jupiter Inlet to the north and immediately adjoining it to the south, Burt Reynolds Jupiter Theatre.

On the attractive grounds of the dinner theatre is a fair-size pond which has been stocked with ducks and some geese and which is constantly visited by a random assortment of winged relations passing by.

Burt Reynolds' ducks, like virtually all birds, are free creatures. We Americans love to boast that we are a free people living in a free land. But compared with our feathererd friends, we know distressingly little about freedom. Take Burt Reynolds' ducks, for instance. Their property line ends a few hundred feet north of their pond where Ocean Parks' begins. But does that concern them? You can bet your $5,000 prize decoy it doesn't! They couldn't care less about property lines — or any other lines, for that matter.

Now it is true they may not care, but I have to tell you that some of our neighbors at Ocean Parks (which is where Isabel and I have our winter home) do. You see, Burt's ducks love to walk across and visit us, which is friendly of them, but a bit messy too. After all, pigeons are not the only birds that like to leave calling cards.

Still and all, I will be glad to serve as attorney for the defense and will argue the case for our theatrical visitors on the grounds of freedom. I hold this truth to be self-evident: that all ducks are created free. Obviously they hold the same view. Since these are domesticated ducks, their flight plans have to be somewhat curtailed, but even so they waddle around the immediate area with a blithe disregard for borders and boundaries. Sad to say, they sometimes waddle a little too carelessly out onto route A-1-A and there some of them have paid freedom's ultimate price.

Even so, I say this in requiem, they have known true liberty. And how many of us reading this obituary and thinking foolish ducks can say the same. Seldom if ever do we humans realize what constrained and constricted lives we lead. And the irony is that the limitations are mostly of our own making. On every side we are bound by ethnic, cultural, racial, religious, national and an exasperating assortment of other people-made walls. We are prisoners of prejudice and hostages to our own mindless misconceptions. We say this is a free world, but we certainly do not live in it as though it were. What we fail to realize is that there are many more kinds of independence than political freedom, which is the kind we think of most often.

For instance, let's suppose you are an engineer. Splendid. But don't fail to get to know and enjoy the perfectly entrancing world of the arts. An artist? Then let me introduce you to Dr. Einstein and the absolutely mind-boggling world of modern physics.

Or consider this question: How many of us Protestants know more than a few Jews and Roman

Catholics? How many of us have attended services and opened our minds and hearts to the ancient beauties, values, wisdoms of Judaism and Catholicism?

How many of us whites have black, Hispanic or Asiatic friends and, by so doing, have generously expanded the horizons of our lives? The spirit, verve, color of other life styles; the eye-opening new ways of viewing the world; the exhilarating sense of discovering the diversity and endless attractiveness of the human race: why, these are discoveries more richly endowed with meaning than Columbus'.

In every sizeable city in this country the world is represented in miniature. There are Greek, Italian, Arabic, Polish, Finnish, Lithuanian, Czechoslovakian, Chinese, etc. neighborhoods. I'll bet New York City has a Patagonian and a Sudanese neighborhood. Engaging people with fascinating cultures. Not to know them is our substantial loss.

The expansive truth is that when we break down or climb over our silly little people-made walls we are enthralled by the sun-bright world that opens before us. Burt Reynolds' ducks may not be the smartest creatures on earth, but they are still more savvy than many of us. Because — you probably don't know this — but "quack" is the duck word for — "freedom."

"You Are What You Think"

Some years ago a new book appeared and affixed itself to the best-seller lists for an enviable stay. Its title? **You Are What You Eat.** That seemed to me an indisputable statement and I had to agree with it. My only objection was that every time I looked in my mirror I thought it a somewhat unflattering commentary on my food.

The title, however, did serve a nobler purpose. For obvious reasons, it set me to reflecting upon one of the plainest and wisest of all truisms: You are what you think. Or as the Bible puts it, "As a man thinketh in his heart, so is he." Or as Marcus Aurelius wrote, "The happiness of your life depends upon the quality of your thoughts." Or as one of our contemporaries has said, "You are not what you think you are; you are what you think."

However and whenever they were stated, these five words have more relevance for our getting-more-out-of-life theme than almost any other five one can think of. For it is implacably true that we do tend to become like and are formed and fashioned by the kind of thoughts that habitually occupy our minds.

All of us understand this principle where food and the body are concerned (though many of us don't do anything about it). Through a process called metabolism, the food we eat literally builds and maintains our bodies. What we also need to understand is that thoughts are the nutrients of the mind and build the mental muscle, agility and substance on which our lives as human beings depend.

Remember **My Fair Lady**? (I don't know why I ask; how could anybody forget it?) That musical marvel was adapted from a keen-witted play by George Bernard Shaw called **Pygmalion.** The play in turn was based on an amusing legend about a man named Pygmalion who took a woman named Galatea and tried to shape her, as a sculptor might shape a piece of clay, into a particular image he had in mind.

We are not aware of the process, but continually you and I are doing the very same thing with ourselves. Some people believe in fate as a, or the, determinant of human destiny. They would do better to look to the quality of the ideas and ideals that mold their minds. As he usually did, Shakespeare said it best, "The fault, dear Brutus, is not in our stars, but in ourselves, that we are underlings."

I have a friend who writes a good deal of popular verse. She has a bit of doggerel called "On Talking to Yourself" which begins, "Be careful what you tell yourself/because you may not know/how much you listen to yourself/are you your friend or foe?" Not Olympian poesy perhaps, but at least it's a tricky way of saying that, more than we know, all of us talk to ourselves, and the things that we say to ourselves in the privacy of our own beings do more to determine our lives than almost any other factor. If people really are what they think, to judge by the living results, many of us are doing some pretty punk thinking.

We children of the twentieth century are justifiably proud of what we have discovered about the microcosm of the atom and the macrocosm of the universe. But in practical, living-life-effectively terms, we ought to be just as pleased with what we have found out about ourselves. During the past century, we have learned what devastating things negative, depressive, destructive thoughts and emotions can do to the human psyche when they persist very long. Conversely, we now know what effect their opposites — positive, outgoing, solicitous sentiments and ideas — can have in a wonderfully affirmative way. More people poison themselves by what they think than by what they drink. Vastly more people find happiness and contentment by what they hold in their minds than by what they hold in their bank accounts.

These statements may sound like some of the most shopworn of cliches and platitudes, and it's true that the basic postulate involved here has received a lot of superficial treatment lately. Still, the only trouble with cliches is not that they aren't valid, often they are profoundly true; the problem is we have handled them so much we have worn off their meaning, familiarity has bred, not so much contempt as disregard.

Perhaps what we should do is look at these words as though we were seeing them for the first time. Think about them. Be struck by the shock of recognition. Let their implications for our lives sink in. For what we have here is one of the most dynamic and salutary of psychological principles.

And if their seemingly simplistic cast still bothers you, if you like a little more convoluted and abstruse statement, how about this: You existentially explicate what you cogitate, meditate and ruminate.

Life Must Have Meaning

Perhaps the darkest chapter in the history of Western civilization is the story of the Nazi concentration camps during the Second World War. It is a story of unparalleled atrocities and unmitigated hell. Yet out of that Holocaust came one of the most illuminating and helpful insights of our time. Incredibly, here is how it happened.

During the past few decades Victor E. Frankl has been one of Europe's leading psychiatrists. An original genius, his work has been acclaimed throughout the world. But in a very different day forty plus years ago this same man was a concentration camp prisoner, apparently condemned to death.

As fate would have it, he was assigned to a work detail and somehow he managed to survive for four absolutely nightmarish years. During them he suffered unmerciful torment. His food was only a crust of bread a day or maybe a cup of very thin soup; he performed the harshest kind of physical labor outdoors in zero temperatures with only rags to cover his body and his broken shoes constantly crammed with snow and ice. Yet even so he fared better than millions of his fellow Jews whom he saw marched off to gas chambers.

When you read his story, you wonder how Dr. Frankl and a handful of others like him were ever able to survive what they did. A few of them lived; most of them died. Why? What made the difference? The answer to that question is the great secret or discovery of Victor Frankl's life.

What is more, he gave us the answer in a single sentence. Dr. Frankl concluded that those people were most likely to survive who had found some real honest-to-God meaning in life. They were men and women who had discovered something so deep, supportive and sustaining that they could survive even the living hell of Auschwitz and Buchenwald. On the basis of his experience in the concentration camps, Victor Frankl became convinced that people are likely to fall sick emotionally, and give up hope, and even die when life loses any authentic meaning for them. Or to put the matter a more positive way, he concluded that our most basic human need is a need for real meaning in life.

First of all, he recognized that those people who did manage to survive were persons who deeply and truly loved. He found that love was a strength, power, force that literally kept them alive. In his own case, Dr. Frankl did not know whether his wife was still living. (As it turned out, his entire family, except for one sister, perished in the gas chambers.) But he has said that just thinking about his wife and all the ineffably precious things she meant to him was as life-sustaining as the food he ate.

Secondly, he concluded that those people were most likely to survive who had values — strong, supportive moral, social and religious values — to live by. These gave their lives a special kind of strength and stability.

Next, he found the survivors were people who kept their minds constantly active and alert. They played word games, did mathematical problems, wrote poems, plays, whole books. Via the magic of memory, Dr. Frankl took long walks and imaginatively recreated every tree and house along the way.

This man had learned all over again one of the most dauntless truths about human life: that while we are not always free to do what we want to, still we are free to choose our attitude, no matter what may happen to us. He wrote, "I may not be free to direct and control all the things that happen to me, but I am free to direct and control my attitude toward those things." What we are talking about here is the ultimate human freedom, and nobody can take it from us, and it means that by choosing our attitudes toward life and constantly re-enforcing them, we **can** prevail, no matter what may happen to us.

So impressed was Dr. Frankl with what he had learned about human nature and survival that he founded a major psychiatric theory on it. He called his theory logotherapy because, among other usages, **logos** was the ancient Greek word for meaning. Like a flower growing out of a noxious swamp, this was the brave and beautiful revelation that grew out of the unimaginable torment of the death camps of Nazism. Its message for all of us is simply this: we will get more of everything out of life, when we find real and enduring meaning in life.

Yin-Yang

China with its one billion people has approximately one fifth of the earth's population today. It also has a civilization as old as its population is big. For the better part of four thousand years the Chinese have viewed life and the world in a singularly pragmatic, common-sensical, down-to-earth fashion. We should not be surprised that it was they who gave us one of mankind's most elemental insights, the grand universal concept of Yin-Yang.

Yin-Yang is a word, but it is also a symbol. You have seen it many times, though you may not have realized what it was. It looks like two inverted teardrops, one black, the other white, the two of them together composing a perfect circle.

In China for millenia now Yin-Yang has symbolized the complimentary dualism or harmony that is basic in the universe. There is day and there is night. There is summer and there is winter. There are hot and cold, body and spirit, life and death. And there is Yin, the female principle, and Yang, the male principle. But none of them is separate or complete in itself; there are simply two sides of one coin, two phases of the same year. There are not really summer **and** winter, life **and** death, there is summer-winter, life-death. There is, in short, an interrelatedness of all things; we are all part of the total organic pattern of the cosmos.

It is not for nothing that we call the vastness in

which we live a universe, meaning an all-encompassing oneness. It is right and proper that we chose to name this nation of ours the **United** States of America. To maintain that bond, we even fought a ghastly fratricidal war. It is profoundly revealing that one of the words and/or concepts we prize most highly is **unity** which means the state of being combined with others to form a greater whole. Universe . . . united . . . unity: They all mean essentially the same thing and that is a fundamental oneness which we celebrate in religion as monotheism, in philosophy as monism and in science as the evidence it has established that the entire cosmos is made up of the very same elements that compose our tiny earth.

One of the great persisting errors of Western civilization is that it has tended to see the world not as Yin-Yang but in terms of mutually exclusive opposites: heaven **and** earth, God **and** man, and, increasingly here in the modern world, man **and** nature. That we are of the earth earthy, that we are as much a part of nature as the gull, the spruce tree, the sea anemone, or the sea itself — this we do not know nor no longer even feel. Nature to us is just one more thing to be used, exploited and overcome. It is as separate from and unrelated to us, we seem to believe, as the latest plastic convenience we have fabricated.

We know a lot, we moderns, about many things: we have accumulated knowledge beyond imagining, but we are not wise men and women. We have discovered marvelous truths, but they are the "truths" of the laboratory and the physics text. It is at once our triumph and our tragedy that we comprehend the scientific, technological truths, but we do not understand Yin-Yang, which may be the simplest and most basic truth of all. And we do not understand it because we do not feel it . . . which is the only way, really, to understand it.

If one of us were to go on a pilgrimmage to a Chinese village and see an old sage sitting by the side of the road and say to him, "Master Kung" (that was the Chinese name for Confucius), "I know there is meaning to life, but I also know there is mystery, sometimes much mystery. On my darkness, can you shed any light?", I think the old man would smile benignly and nod in the way one fancies Chinese sages nodding and simply say, "Yin-Yang."

How Much Can You Stand?

There is an ancient fable about an old man who one day was walking down a long road with a great bundle of sticks on his back. Finally, overcome with weariness and discouragement, he sank down by the side of the road and said with a groan that he wished he were dead.

Immediately, to his surprise and terror, Death appeared before him and asked him what he would like to have. With astonishing alacrity, the old man sprang to his feet and exclaimed, "I wish to have my bundle on my back and my feet once more on the road."

The old man had discovered that things were not so bad but what they couldn't be worse, and that, although he would never have thought so a minute before, he still had the strength to carry on. He had found out that he really could stand a good deal more than he ever thought he could.

I expect this is a universal assumption: that there are limits to the amount of sorrow and suffering we can take. It does seem reasonable, certainly. And it would appear equally logical to assume that there are no limits to the amount of pleasure and satisfaction we can handle.

Yet, believe it or not, the evidence of human experience indicates that we have our facts reversed here, and, unlikely as this may sound, that we can cope with handicaps and hardships more capably than we can with long-range indolence and inactivity.

The surprising truth about passive pleasure and languid contentment is that there seems to be a saturation point beyond which we become surfeited, just as we do when we eat too much candy, or any other food, for that matter. Pleasure would seem to be something that is best taken in moderate doses. Give a person too much food, drink, sleep, play, vacation and he will soon become restive, jaded, frustrated.

My wife and I learned this hardy truth the way we human beings learn so many things, through experience. Dreaming of sun, sand and sea, we had planned a month-long winter vacation down in the Virgin Islands. And, sure enough, the first week was everything we had hoped for. The second week was somewhat less so. By the end of the third week, we had had such a fill of simply lying in the sand and splashing in the sea that — if you can believe this — we had our tickets changed and flew home a week early!

Toward the end of our stay, lazing in the sun, I remember pondering the great lesson the eminent English scholar Arnold Toynbee learned from his lifelong study of history. He concluded that periodically a civilization has to be stoutly challenged, it has to face difficulty, danger, mortal peril, otherwise there is almost certain to be a slackening of spirit, a weakening of will, a general decline. Nations, he maintained, can endure hardship and danger more effectually than they can long-range prosperity and abundance. This was his famous "challenge and response" theory.

Whether we are talking about people or nations, the truth seems to be that there are tolerance points or maximum capacities where idle pleasure and bovine contentment are concerned, but not necessarily when hardship, difficulty and danger are involved. Here are two questions. Number one: What do you want life to do to or for you? And, number two: What do you want to do with life? If you want it to give you unearned satisfactions and unwarranted pleasures; if you want life simply to dish it out so that you can lackadaisically enjoy it without stress or strain or struggle, your tolerance point is going to be reached pretty fast.

On the other hand, if you want to assume the initiative and do things with life instead of being done to, if you are willing to say to life, Go ahead, challenge me! Give me some really tough problems and difficult jobs and against them let me test the measure of my strength and will and spirit — talk in these terms and I do not think you will need to worry about your ability to take it or where that power may come from.

The title of this little piece is "How Much Can You Stand?"

I guess the answer is: as much as you have to.

The Magic of Memory

It was one of those supernally lovely summer days that occasionally can and do occur almost everywhere. But down on the coast of Maine there seems to be a special poignancy and enthrallment about them. Perhaps this is so because the season is short there; summer is little more than two months long; a man knows such days are few and fleeting, and when they come he feels their balm with a curious urgency and eagerness.

In any event, from sunrise to sunset the beauty of this flawless day had utterly captivated my wife and me. We were wandering along the coast in our little cabin cruiser Gypsy. The breeze out of the southwest was a gentle ten knots and the waters of the North Atlantic all around us danced and sparkled as though in celebration of such a day. I have never seen that water bluer or the sky as blue. The light was so crystalline clear I felt as though I could see to the end of the world and it warmed our bodies and spirits the whole day long.

Toward evening as the sun was setting in a blaze of crimson glory behind the darkling green of the Camden hills, we put into a little fishing port for the night. And suddenly I felt a twinge of sadness. I thought to myself, What a perfect day this has been. It's the sort a man dreams of through long winter nights. How sad that such a day has to end and all this beauty be so evanescent.

And then, as swiftly, another thought occurred to

me. But this day doesn't have to end, my mind triumphantly reminded me. I can keep it alive forever — through the magic of memory! This sunlight and skyscape, this sea breeze and blue water, this salt spray blowing free — these are mine to have and to cherish as long as I live. The meaning is memory and memory is the secret.

I don't talk to myself very often, but when I do I wish I could always be as sensible and sagacious. For I was profoundly right: of all our many blessings, what is dearer than memory. It resurrects and brings back to us our loved ones who have slipped away. It recreates the enchanted places and all the glorious sights and sounds of eye and ear. And it enables us to live over again the peak experiences of our lives. Alexander Smith may have overstated the case a bit, but forgivably so; he said, "A man's real possession is his memory. In nothing else is he rich, in nothing else is he poor." Other epigrammatists have played with the same conceit contending that the most beautiful lives are those that create the most beautiful memories. Naturally, the latter following logically from the former.

However mawkish these sentiments maybe sometimes sound, you have to concede their essential truth. Youth has few memories of its own; it must create them, and that is best done before the sun moves too far west. What youth cannot know is that its most exuberant experiences, those rapturous occasions undimmed by failure or regret, are a food that feeds the soul in later years as perhaps nothing else can. Oscar Wilde, who cherished memory as every prisoner must, said, "Memory is the diary that we all carry about with us."

But it is more than that, even. It is a way of living vicariously as we can no longer live after we have dropped too many quarters in the toll booth of time. (Now there's an epigram that may linger in your memory — whether you want it to or not.)

I am discovering that the trouble with writing about memory is trying to avoid the platitudinous. I want to say that old age has few compensations, but that memory is one of them. (It is also true that every cloud has a silver lining and that this too shall pass away.) Possibly it is because we tend to romanticize our memories that there seems to be a slightly sweet — sometimes bittersweet — flavor about them. That perfect Maine coast day — perhaps the sea wasn't quite as blue or the wind as fresh or the light as pellucid as I remember them.

But does it matter? Indeed, what we unconsciously do may be a salutary thing. Old age needs all the lightness and brightness it can get. And if gilding a few lilies and touching up an album of faded recollections helps, if a sunnier past can come to the aid of a more somber present, why then let memory play its tricks and bless it for the doing.

On second thought, I want to rescind a statement I made a moment ago. That utterly idyllic summer day — maybe memory plays tricks most of the time and makes the sun shine brighter than suns can shine. But I swear **that** day, **that** sea, **that** woman I was with, ignore everything I've just been saying: It was all that I have said it was, no less and conceivably even more, it was what I would have to call . . . an epiphany.

"To Believe in the Heroic Makes Heroes"

Two of the most distinguished men of letters of the 19th century were Thomas Carlyle, an Englishman, and Ralph Waldo Emerson, an American. In 1832, they met in England for the first of two visits, became fast friends and began what evolved into a famous lifelong correspondence.

One of a number of qualities they shared and relished was their faith in the ability of great men to shape history. They were two disciples who believed in heroes. At the beginning of **Representative Men,** Emerson said, "It is natural to believe in great men. All mythology opens with demigods." And in his **Heroes and Hero Worship,** Carlyle enthused, "Great men taken up in any way are profitable company. We cannot look, however imperfectly, upon a great man without gaining something by him."

Heroes have rather gone out of fashion in our day and certainly the word worship is no longer indicated. As realists rather than idealists, we are wary of the deadfalls and delusions to which hero worshippers are likely prey. Still and all, weren't Emerson and Carlyle on to a major truth about a universal human need or longing? Consciously to expose ourselves to the influence of great men and women: Isn't that about as wise and formative a practice as any of us can follow? Let us see.

Whether or not we realize this, all of us tend to

model ourselves after other people, the son after the father, the daughter after the mother. It's a responsibility awesome enough to frighten any parent right out of his or her wits. Perhaps the role model is a teacher, coach, personal friend, business associate, political figure. Fine. But now why not go on and through our reading, studying, reflecting get to know, and in the process be influenced by, some of history's immortals? Who they may be is up to us. But one thing is certain: there is no more effective way to play the great American game of self-improvement. We do this, not by slavish imitation, but by the contagion and inspiration of worthwhile influence.

We ought also to recognize that, judging from abundant evidence, everybody **needs** heroes. Deep within the human psyche, there seems to be an inexpungible longing for such guides and mentors. If our culture does not provide them, we create them. Davy Crockett, Daniel Boone, Old Bill Williams, Kit Carson were tolerable creations. But what are we to say about Elvis Presley, Michael Jackson, Madonna, Prince? (Whatever it is, please don't say it.)

Well, we mustn't belabor the point: People require heroes because we mortals wander down a road on which signposts are scarce and we need all the advisements and directions we can get. Heroes point the way and they motivate us to walk in it. We may never reach Achilles' Happy Isles, but at least we now have a better sense of where they are.

Too, we should recognize that history's illustrious souls provide us with something else all of us need, a standard of excellence. Always there is a plethora of talk in our schools, churches and (sometimes) homes about goodness, greatness, nobility, character, love and assorted admirable virtues. But these are likely to be pretty abstract concepts unless we can tie them down and attach them to flesh-and-blood realities. When we do, they come alive, are defined and embodied. In our American tradition, who better exemplifies nobility than Washington? character than Lee? magnanimity than Lincoln? compassion than Clara Barton? leadership than Roosevelt? statesmanship than General Marshall? Men and women of their calibre not only demonstrate that greatness is possible, they show us in living color and heroic action what greatness is like. They give us what all of us desperately need: people we can believe in and seek to be like. They help us understand that "Heroism is philosophy teaching by example."

A man who was arguably Britain's most able Prime Minister, Benjamin Disraeli, offered this advice: "Nurture your mind with the great thoughts of great men; to believe in the heroic makes heroes." It certainly helps. We do tend to become like what we believe in. Or as Goethe said, "We are shaped and fashioned by what we love." Is there a finer way to make more of our lives than to expose them to the heroic, and by so doing, in the process, to take unto ourselves something of heroism's gentleness and strength, and of its everlasting mercy.

How Is Your Viability?

Haiti, a strange and haunted country, is, appropriately, the home of voodoo, a strange and outlandish religion. It is a mythology full of black magic, charms and sorcery, evil spells and witch doctors, and the devil only knows what else.

Among other oddities, voodoo is the religion that believes in zombies. Zombies are animated dead men. They haven't been brought back to life, quite, but they are corpses that can be made to walk and move about. If you are not careful down in Haiti, some black night in the dark of the moon you are likely to meet a zombie, a dead man walking.

Myself, I have been fortunate in my visits there; I have never encountered a single zombie. But, sad to say, I have not been so lucky back here at home because in this enlightened land where we don't believe in such things, I have met quite a few zombies — and it hasn't been in the dark of the moon either!

The medical and legal professions would have you believe that people are either dead or alive, but personally I think that's much too arbitrary a judgment. I think this business of "aliveness" is a highly relative matter for I have known some people who are 95% alive most of the time and I have known others who are 75% dead much of the time — dead, that is, in terms of their responses, interests, enthusiasms and contributions to life. It is quite possible, you know, to die at 40 and not be buried until 80. Henry Mencken claimed he found the human race to consist largely of healthy bodies staggering around under the weight of dead minds.

Well, enough of such morbidity. The key to what I am getting at here is found in a single word not commonly used, "viability." Viability obviously derives from the Latin and according to Mr. Webster it means "the ability to live, grow and develop."

There are two scientists who make a profession of studying life, the biologist and the psychologist. One studies the life of the body, the other the life of the psyche, and both agree that few things are more important in this world than viability, or the capacity for living, growing and developing. There is little question that the happiest, the most richly contented people, the ones who get the most out of life, are the people who have a maximum degree of viability, of this aptitude for joyful, creative living. Maybe I should have called this particular piece "Are You a Heliotrope?" Heliotropism is the natural turning of plants toward the sun. That's what some fortunate people also instinctively do.

One reason we have never sufficiently appreciated the seemingly obvious truth involved here is that for most of us the word "alive" or "aliveness" has a wholly physical connotation. We say a person is alive as long as he is breathing and his heart is beating; he is dead when the heart stops. This is entirely a physical matter.

As I am using the word, however, it has a different sort of meaning. A psychical or spiritual, not physical one. By spiritual aliveness I mean a certain inner vitality; an eager, outgoing responsiveness of one's whole being; a sustaining sense of security and tranquility; a **joie de vivre** that nothing can permanently blight. If the fates were to grant me only one wish, I think this would be it: that to the end of my days I might be capable of living and drinking life to the full and rejoicing in it, no matter how rough the going might get.

Rufus Babcock must have had something of this sort in mind when he said, "Life is what we are alive to. It is not length, but breadth. To be alive only to appetite, pleasure, pride and money-making, and not to goodness and kindness, purity and love, poetry, music, flowers, stars, God and eternal hopes — why, this is to be all but dead!"

So — what must we do? We must take every care that we do not die before our time, becoming spiritual zombies, still breathing and walking and talking perhaps, but dead inside where it really counts. The wisest thing you and I can do is stay alive — as long as we live!

Fervently, I agree with the anonymous sage who said, "To die is a small thing, for sooner or later death must come to all of us. But to live — **truly** to live — is a very large thing, for this is a secret only the most favored of men and women really know."

Sometimes when you have to, when you must, say No.

But when you speak to life always, **always,** say — Yes!

The Man Who Found His Answer

If I had to choose one book that represents what is best, most original and most characteristically American in our literature, I think I would choose Henry Thoreau's **Walden.** Hemingway came out with his dukes up fighting for **Huckleberry Finn,** and I wouldn't protest the decision, but I still put my money on **Walden.**

It is a singular book, but one familiar to most of us. Henry David Thoreau was a prickly, iconoclastic young fellow who lived in Concord, Massachusetts in the first half of the last century when Concord really was the Athens of America. His best friend was Ralph Waldo Emerson for whom he served as a sort of handyman-companion and from whom he learned priceless lessons in writing and thinking.

But fortunate as his lot may have been, Henry hankered after something odd, and, it seemed, eccentric. Most people, he believed, "live lives of quiet desperation." He wanted to find out if life couldn't be lived with a little more surety, harmony, openness of sense and spirit. The man was not particularly antisocial or misogynistic, as most of his fellow villagers thought, but there was in him a restless hunger for communion with something more than simply human beings. He wanted to feel his organic relationship with the whole of life. He wanted to get better acquainted with the universe.

So Henry made his Great Decision. He decided to go out to Walden Pond only a few miles from Concord, in those days a wild place surrounded by pitch pine, hemlock and laurel, and bustling with all sorts of wildlife. There, at a cost of $28.12, he built himself a little one-room cabin in which he lived from 1845 to 1847.

People wondered why a man would do such a seemingly misanthropic thing. Here's one delightful reason: because, as he said, he wanted to be a self-appointed inspector of snow-storms, huckleberry patches and woodchuck holes. A more sober reason was this: "I went to the woods because I wished to live deliberately, to front only the essential facts of life and see if I could not learn what it had to teach, and not when I came to die, discover that I had not lived." Since the title of our book is what it is, I hope you will not think I am being self-serving when I baldly say that Thoreau went to Walden to learn how to get more out of life. There is no way of stating his intent more clearly or directly.

All of which brings us to his masterpiece, one of only two of the books he wrote which were published in his lifetime. At a surface level, **Walden** is a report of one man's two-year stay at a woodland pond. But at a deeper level, it is an account by an extremely sensitive and perceptive spirit who had a divine gift for language of how he saw beneath the surface of the pond to the continuous wonders of creation; of how he experienced nature as a universal, but also personal, reality; of how he lived wholly and sucked out the marrow of life.

Henry felt that most of us do not get full value out of our mortal stay. Instead, our lives are all cluttered up with unnecessary, often foolish detail. "Simplify, simplify," he fairly shouted. Get down to basics. "It is life near the bone where it is sweetest." We live surrounded by sextillions of miracles and we see them not.

Don't misunderstand him. **Walden** is no fatuous, quixotic treatise inveigling all of us to go off and live by ourselves in the woods at Walden Pond. What Thoreau **is** saying is that we ought to discover and get to know our own real selves and trust those selves and be truly independent and live life more fully and keenly and deeply. Before it is too late (Thoreau died at the age of forty-five), we had better wake up and live, else we are likely to come to the end of our lives to realize belatedly that we had never really lived at all.

This is the way he said it: "If the day and the night are such that you greet them with joy, and life emits a fragrance like flowers and sweet-scented herbs, is more elastic, more starry, more immortal — that is your success."

If You Had Your Life to Live Over Again

Reincarnation seems not to be a widely held belief in our culture, as we have observed elsewhere in these pages. Do people feel that one time around the track is sufficient, or do they fear that the second time around might be even rougher than the first? — who knows.

Still, it's a tempting thought. Suppose you really could live your life over again, what would you attempt to say, do, be? For surely none of us believes that he has touched all the bases in the first game, or has gathered all the daisies in the meadow. A second chance! What a fascinating thought — and one that is not quite as preposterous as it probably sounds.

Of course there are always the infidels who argue that since, presumably, we would have the same genetic make-up and the same environmental background, we would turn out pretty much the same pedestrian way we did on the first go-around. But give us credit, please, for learning at least a smidgen from experience and for being a little sadder/wiser on the return trip. So let's play this game of Second Time Around and see where we might reasonably expect to come out.

It is nice, and not implausible, to assume that this time we would be a little more objective about and honest with ourselves. All of us have an assortment of small (and sometimes not so small!) faults and failings. Most of them are correctable, or at least improvable. If only each of us would recognize these weaknesses of ours for what they are and would seek redress, the effort could work wonders in our lives. We need simply add a single word to a familiar maxim and say, "Self-honesty is the best policy."

Next, the odds are big that most of us would try to get a whale of a lot more out of life a second time around. Money is not the answer. Neither is a stack of stuff that turns out to be only silver-plated at best. But the wise use of time and opportunity may very well be. And those opportunities are all around us. People for love and friendship. Work to be done that can be creative and satisfying. Hobbies, sports, skills to pursue and develop. The world of nature to know and rejoice in. Good causes to give our help to, which, in turn, will give their blessing to us. And challenges of every sort to strengthen the mettle of our spirits and make us feel more intensely alive than we otherwise do.

One of the real tragedies of human experience is that most of us do not take sufficient advantage of our good fortune or of the opportunities for enrichment and fulfillment that surround all but the most luckless of us. "A fool," it has been said, "is a person who does not learn from experience." "What fools," it has also been said, "these mortals be."

One of the pieces in this book describes procrastination as the eighth deadly sin. Because the term means more than simply putting things off; it means wasting time. And time, as Franklin knew, is our most precious commodity. "Waste not time, for time is the stuff that life is made of."

If our own second coming were really to occur and we looked in sorrow at all the things we hadn't done, the places we hadn't visited, the opportunities we hadn't seized, the friends we hadn't kept in touch with, the words we hadn't spoken, the challenges we hadn't faced up to — if this were to happen, don't you agree that our second life passage for most of us would be appreciably better, fuller, finer than the first.

Finally, isn't it plausible to believe that during a repeat performance we might show a little more respect for the authentic, enduring values of human life and less for the meretricious ones that seduce so many of us. Would it be money in the bank, name in the paper and fair-weather friends? Or would it be a residue of kindnesses remembered, wisdom, quietly, daily manifested, and love so consistently lived that it seemed as ordinary as those other wonders, sunshine and starlight?

All this second-time-around talk sounds like the sheerest kind of nonsense, of course. But is it, really? We have all heard that worn-to-pieces cliche, "Today is the first day of the rest of your life." Well, forget its seeming banality. Recognize its irrefutable truth. Consider taking this game seriously, after all, and saying, From now I am going to live my life as though I really had been given a second chance. I am going to attempt to say and do and be the sort of person I should have been in the past and now know I can be in the future.

Reincarnation? Maybe not in the usually accepted sense. But to make of the rest of one's life what could so worthily be made would be a mighty fine substitute indeed.

45

Our Mother, the Earth

In the wondrous world of Greek mythology there is a story about a giant from Libya named Antaeus. Apparently he was a rather fractious fellow because whenever a stranger entered his country, he would compel the visitor to wrestle with him. Actually, Antaeus may have been more cantankerous than courageous for, truth to tell, he possessed a secret that rendered him virtually unbeatable. In his wrestling bouts, even if his opponents did manage to throw him, the giant derived fresh strength whenever he touched his mother, the earth, and so he remained invincible.

As is so often the case with Greek mythology, there is an easily discerned parallel here — or should it be parable? — with our modern situation. Whether we realize it or not, we draw from the earth a primordial strength and support and security that are as old as life itself; and when we lose that contact we are cut off from the physical, and more than physical, roots of our being as surely as the great pine is ravished when the hurricane rips up and destroys its roots.

Because, you see, the rest of that old Greek legend is this: Antaeus was at last defeated only when he lost contact with the earth. One day Heracles in combat with him discovered the secret of the giant's strength, and lifting his opponent high in the air, he crushed him to death.

The moral here, I suspect, is that we may hold our

heads in the clouds, but we had better keep our feet on the earth. For deep in the souls of us moderns is a longing and a lostness. It is really a kind of hunger for the only way and the only world our progenitors had ever known. It was a world of plants and trees and animals, of many waters and familiar stars, of mountains dark against setting suns and of prairies innocent and endless in dawn's first light, of time measured by moons and of distance determined by hills and valleys. It was a world of sap and sinew and blood and life in which everything was of the earth earthy, coming from it and returning to it, a world that man and proto-man had known for a million years, a green and growing natural world now gone, or almost so, for modern man and woman.

It is true, of course, that we do have an incredible aptitude for adaptation, invention and (sometimes) cooperation. This capacity has enabled us to create language, develop society, form government, build great cities, perfect technology and fly to the moon. It has produced what we call civilization, the most astonishing phenomenon in all the universe — as far as we yet know. Let no one disparage or despise it. We were animals once. We are human beings now. And along with our secret aspirations and our divine potential, it has made us what we are.

But, after all, we have lived in our cities, where most Americans now dwell (city, a word that comes from the same root as civilization) only a few weeks as anthropological time is measured. We forget that people, like trees, have roots, and when those roots go down into the earth millions of years deep, we cannot sever them without affecting our spirit's health. Without feeling sickness of a sort. I wonder if it isn't a kind of homesickness we suffer from . . .

If you accept this primal fact, you should not be surprised to learn that to the former occupants of our country (I did not say owners because the Indians did not believe that anyone owned the earth) the land had a kind of religious significance. All primitive religions are nature religions. Among a good many other definitions, my dictionary says that primitive means original and primary. All religions try to get back to origins. For what they just instinctively, naturally did, you have to give the Indians eagle-high marks.

At an annual meeting of the American Association for the Advancement of Science some years ago, the historian Lynn White, Jr. pleaded for a new attitude toward human nature and destiny. The only hope for the world's salvation, he contended, is the nurturing on our part of the same sentient, empathetic feeling that St. Francis and his followers had for the physical and spiritual interdependence of all elements of nature. Then White went on to maintain that scientists today ought to take as their patron saint, of all people, Saint Francis of Assisi!

With the Greeks, with the Indians, with all sensitive men and women everywhere, can't we agree that you and I have what amounts to a religious obligation to tend and respect and love our mother, the earth. For out of her dust we came and back to her dust we shall go. Without her we would not have been, and — children of the nuclear age, remember this — without her we shall not be.

The Reality Principle

One of the most recent of the world's major sciences is psychiatry. It is the science or the practice of treating mental illness. As such, it is an exceedingly complex and difficult, and sometimes confusing and murky, subject. Yet if it had to be reduced to a few simple words, we could say that as much as anything else psychiatry is concerned with the reality principle. It is no great exaggeration to declare that this principle, or our many and subtle attempts to defy it, is what psychiatry is chiefly concerned with.

By the phrase, all psychiatry means is the ability to see ourselves as we really are and the world as it actually is. In other words, it is our capacity for accepting reality. Here is another of those truths about the human condition so obvious it would seem to be self-evident. Yet nothing causes more trouble in our lives than our hopeless attempts to violate this principle and to try to escape what simply cannot be avoided.

It may help us if we look at the obverse side of the matter and understand that the mentally ill, particularly those who are seriously ill, have difficulty in accepting reality. They think of themselves as being more inferior and unworthy than they actually are; falsely they see people as being suspicious or contemptuous of them; they fantasize and hallucinate; and if they are psychotic, they may lose all contact with reality and live alone in a strange, grotesque world of illusion and make-believe.

I have a friend who used to write a good deal on mental health and related matters. He sometimes facetiously remarked that he liked to daydream because he met a better class of people that way. It was an amusing line, and actually it had some validity. There are times when we ought legitimately to escape. Vacations, sports, movies, parties, the reading of detective, science fiction, romance and adventure stories, these are all perfectly acceptable retreats from the harrying demands of everyday life. From the point of view of personal well-being, it is of major importance that we know how to escape when we really need to and ought to.

But beyond a point quickly reached we have to come back from playland and fantasy world and live with the rough and rigorous demands of our day-to-day world, whether we like it as it is or not. In fact the principal effort of psychiatry is to help people find their way back to the real world again.

By contrast with his disturbed friend, the mentally healthy person has both feet planted squarely on the solid ground of reality. He has an honest understanding both of his own abilities and his own shortcomings, and he knows about what he ought sensibly to expect from other people and from life itself. Such a person has the wisdom to know himself and to accept the truth about himself, for he realizes that truth, or, as we are calling it here, reality, is the only foundation upon which to build one's life.

A firm grounding in reality also serves as a check to prevent us from doing what we all sometimes feel like doing, and that is quitting and escaping — in the wrong ways. For there are a multitude of bad escape routes available, and some of them are highly ingenious ones. By driving too fast, by drugs and drink, by fantasizing and wishful thinking, by casual affairs that have no substance and no heart, by evading unpleasant facts and refusing to face up to things as they really are: by such devious ways we seek to avoid the inevitable.

Cervantes' Don Quixote is one of the most memorable characters in literature. He is also an affecting symbol of the impossibility of avoiding reality. In an amusing but futile attempt to escape from a world he does not like, he dons his rusty armor, mounts his skinny steed Rosinante, and charges forth into a dreamland where he believes that windmills are giants, inns are castles and flocks of sheep are mighty armies.

Well, much as he might sometimes like to sally forth with Don Quixote, the mentally healthy person stays home to do battle with real giants. The reality principle holds him steady, helps him confront his problems and, if at all possible, overcome them. To accept the world as it is and ourselves as we are may sound like no great achievement, but ask any psychologist or psychiatrist. You will learn there are few greater and none more essential.

At the bitter end, it is the lost-in-illusion-land wanderer, that most piteous of all lost souls, who gets so little out of life. His friend, the person who accepts things as they are and himself as he is, who faces the world without fear or evasion, it is he who dwells on the bright high uplands of reality where dreams, sound and steadfast dreams, may indeed come true.

Life as Adventure

Adventure! What thrilling images the word evokes. Stouthearted men daring uncharted seas . . . Rivers, regions, whole continents, even the polar regions explored and mapped . . . A host of nameless, but not forgotten, pioneers irresistibly moving like a tide across the wilderness to establish a brave new Land of the Free and so fulfill our manifest destiny. Magnificently, they all confirm these words: "Adventure is the poetry of action."

They remind us that up until now much of the human saga has been a real blood-and-guts, doughty-and-daring adventure story. But you notice that qualifying "up to now." Today we Americans live in a world where the wilderness has been reduced to the dimensions of a state park and the only unexplored regions are the places we have not yet visited. Today one can travel for thousands of miles around this country and not have an adventure more exciting than staying at a Howard Johnson's Motor Lodge instead of a Holiday Inn.

Ah, the heroic and romantic past! Sometimes we must feel like that prototype of Kiplingesque, derring-do adventurers, T.E. Lawrence, who mourned that the whole world has now been "explored, boxed in and compassed 'bout." And sometimes as we sit in our air-conditioned office or stand in our standardized home, wistfully it does seem so.

Yet, how foolish of us, really. Whoever maintained that adventure has to be defined in terms of a Douglas

Fairbanks-John Huston-Clint Eastwood movie, that its authentic purpose is to serve as an outlet for rough-and-tough macho virility? Perhaps the time has come when we need a new concept of adventure, not so much physical in a he-man, tough-guy sense as moral and social in a civilizing sense. Adventure as response to honest-to-God challenges worthy of responsible, intelligent, concerned human beings.

So different are they from past patterns of thought and conduct that the following suggestions may seem to have precious little to do with adventure. Yet if my dictionary is right and "adventure is an exciting and remarkable experience," we may be on to something here.

For instance, consider the "exciting and remarkable," not to mention daring and dangerous, event that took place in this country somewhat over two decades ago. At that time the civil rights issue was boiling to an explosive pitch, nowhere more so than in Selma and Birmingham, Alabama. To call attention to the shameful plight of black people there, several thousand men and women from all over the country converged to hold what turned out to be an historic march.

Certainly that march was a response to a challenge, and certainly it required both moral and physical courage. Moreover, the goal sought was assuredly a noble one: to help win the civil rights, presumably guaranteed them by the Constitution, of millions of disenfranchised Americans. What happened that pivotal day has to be called an adventure.

Or consider another contemporary kind of adventure also involving victims of bias and bigotry. Women!

No fair-minded person can deny that through the ages women have suffered a flagrant deal of discrimination, obviously in the job market, but also in scores of other big and little, personal and social ways. It has been an exhilarating, soul-satisfying adventure for women to step out of the kitchen and into the marketplace and impressively establish their claims to equality in the entertainment, sports, academic, business, industrial, political and every other world you can think of.

What about all the projects in your community volunteers have tackled, initially out of a sense of obligation, perhaps, but have ended up with a sense of accomplishment whose other name might again be adventure. Hospice, Planned Parenthood, Red Cross, Urban League, NAACP, World Affairs Council, United Fund, hospitals, juvenile courts, child care centers, senior citizens groups . . . But it's foolish to go on; the list is almost interminable. These kinds of volunteer activities may not seem like and may not necessarily, ipso facto, be adventures. The point is, though: every one of them **can** be.

Perhaps we should let one of the most esteemed philosophers of the twentieth century, Alfred North Whitehead, have the last word. As a scholar, he was sometimes hard to understand, but as a man writing about our universal human experience, he was simplicity itself. Said he, "In their day the great achievements of the past were the great adventures of the past . . . A race preserves its vigor so long as it is nerved by the vigor to adventure beyond the safeties of the past. Without adventure, civilization is in full decay." Amen and amen.

Dog Teaches Man

People love formulas. Simple ones. For finding happiness, or making friends, or achieving success . . . or getting more out of life.

Well, if the latter is your heart's desire, here's as simple and rewarding a formula as you are likely to find, and in only three words at that: get a dog. Or a cat. Or a horse. Or any other warm-blooded creature that appeals to you.

I say dog because dogs are my fancy. To such an extent, in fact, that my wife has become a little concerned. She says I should watch the way in which I unguardedly remark that I like people, but I love dogs. I expect she's right, and I don't think I really mean what I seem to be saying.

But I do mean this. There is no love as precious and ennobling as that of one human being for another. The love we feel for our wife or husband, or our children, or our dearest friends is the most sublime manifestation of the human spirit. It is not so much in thinking or reasoning as in loving that we reach toward the divine.

Still there is one qualification that has to be made here. Human love is seldom, if ever, "pure" in the sense that it is totally free of rationalization and reflection, of doubts and queries. If "I love you" is the most often spoken declaration, "Yes, but how much do you love me?" may be the most often unspoken response. We do sometimes love wholeheartedly, but even then, being human, we are also at the same time pondering, wondering, questioning.

Dogs, by contrast, are not so burdened. They never say, "Who was that other dog I saw you with last night?" They don't wonder, or question, or doubt, or complain. They just plain love. And if that love lacks the depth and dimension of human love, it does have its own unique quality of being always there and always unalloyed.

It is almost impossible to destroy a dog's love. Ignore him, starve him, beat him, still his love endures. Such a response on the part of a human being might well be senseless, unworthy, even craven. But we are talking here about a different kind of creature. What we should expect of a human, we have no right to expect of an animal. All I am making is a simple point: that unqualified love, the sort that asks no questions, makes no demands, has no doubts, is one of life's most uplifting experiences.

When I count my blessings, I place high on the list that wonderfully warm, tail-wagging, whole-hearted love that Sandy and Pepper and Doug and Bruce and, particularly, Frankie have given me. And as for my love for them, let me tell you this. When our beloved 17-year-old poodle Frankie died two years ago, my wife and I were so grief-stricken we couldn't even speak his name for several days. We had known we loved him much, but we had not anticipated the depth of our anguish. Seldom have we grieved more at the death of a cherished friend.

To a person who is not a dog or animal lover, I

suspect this sort of confession may sound absurdly sentimental, a kind of anthropomorphizing carried to a maudlin extreme.

Well, whether it be a silly sentimentality or, as I believe it has been, an illuminating, ongoing experience in pure and simple loving, at least I know this much: that without my canine companions I would never have gotten as much of the joy and fun and affection out of life as I have been privileged to know. They have taught me some lessons in simple, unaffected loving I don't think I could have learned in any other way. People who have dogs understand how much communication goes on between them and their pets. But there may be more, and in more sweet and subtle ways, than even they realize.

The most moving tribute to a dog I have ever read was given us by Lord Byron when his beloved Boatswain died in 1808. Byron wrote this epitaph for that dog:

"Near this spot
Are deposited the remains of one
Who possessed beauty without vanity,
Strength without insolence,
Courage without ferocity
And all the virtues of man without his vices.
This praise, which would be unmeaning flattery
If inscribed over human ashes,
Is but a just tribute to the memory of
Boatswain . . . a dog."

The Eighth Deadly Sin

According to tradition, there are seven deadly sins that bedevil the human race. If you are not up on the subject, let me inform you that these seven sinister savages are pride, covetousness, lust, anger, gluttony, envy and sloth.

Now as if these were not bad enough, I think there is an eighth fault or failing that needs to be added to this misbegotten collection. In fact, I know it. I know it both from my own experience and from that of the human race collectively. You will not be impressed when you hear its name. It sounds as innocuous as sloppiness or tardiness or forgetfulness. But be not deceived, friend, you are looking at a word, or a fault, that causes us to lose more of life's pleasures and satisfactions than almost anything else I can think of. Believe me, I speak with authority. The innocent-sounding name of the culprit is — procrastination.

Procrastinating is something as easy to do as sweeping cracker crumbs under the rug. It is nothing more or less than the practice of putting things off. Of saying, "I'll do that next week." Of genuinely intending to do soon what we ought to do now. Whoever said "The road to hell is paved with good intentions" gets an A + in my class. Spanish speaking people have the perfect word for it, **manana.** Tomorrow. Don't worry, there's always tomorrow. We'll do it then (maybe).

Do you know who the best person is to give you

an impassioned lecture on the subject of procrastination? Anybody over 65. If there is one thing all older people agree about, and bitterly regret, it is the sin of procrastination. I don't care who they are. Take the most successful, the wealthiest, the happiest senior citizen you can find and I guarantee you he or she will echo the old refrain, "Oh, if I had only done this or that or the next thing while there was still time." These may not be the saddest words in the language, but to the person approaching the end of his life and realizing how much he had wanted to do, intended to do, planned to do, but somehow now will never do — I tell you those eighteen simple words are heartbreaking.

In all fairness we should admit that of course no human being can possibly accomplish everything he would like to do. But, you see, we're talking here about the things he could have done and would like to have done, but didn't do. There's a vast difference between the impossible and the possible that was never attempted.

Time, was that the problem? No. It wasn't for lack of time that we didn't write that book we always talked about, or never took a trip abroad, or tried out those exciting new merchandising ideas, or kept in touch with those dear friends who once meant so much to us.

I have just quoted one hoary maxim, now here's another: What people regret most are not their sins of commission, but of omission. Looking back over the course of my life, I have the grace to be embarrassed by more committed sins than I like to recognize. Even so, I think it is the sins of omission, all the things I wanted to do and could have done, but never did, that bother me most. "Dreams come true" is an inadequate statement. What we ought to say is "Dreams come true — when we make them come true." As long as we procrastinate, just that long do we put off the fulfillment of our dreams.

This is why the end result of procrastination is frustration. To live an incompleted, unfulfilled life is to learn what frustration really means. And the sour, sorry thing about it all is that the story didn't have to turn out this empty way. Nobody has ever contended that we have to realize all our hopes and aspirations. We simply have to try. And the sooner the better. Because all of us veteran procrastinators know that the longer we put things off, the less likely we are to do them.

These words do not sound much like Horace Mann, yet in one of his writings he inserted this notice: "Lost! Somewhere between sunrise and sunset: two golden hours. Each set with sixty diamond minutes. No reward is offered because they are gone forever."

Another American wise man, that wily old jack-of-all-trades Benjamin Franklin, put the matter a little more soberly and succinctly when he said, "Dost thou love life? Then waste not time, for time is the stuff that life is made of."

So, class, the moral of today's lesson is this: We can all get more out of life than we have presently found, but we had better start getting **today!**

On Living With Oneself

During the past century and a half the charming little New England college town of Amherst, Massachusetts has been home and haven to a whole covey of poets. Chief among them was a strange, bewitching creature named Emily Dickinson who is frequently regarded today as having been America's leading woman poet. It is an honor she warrants for few poets, men or women, have enjoyed such penetrating insights into nature and human nature or her epigrammatic ability to express ideas in a minimum of perfectly chosen words.

Because she never married, because she spent virtually her entire life in Amherst from 1830 to 1886 rarely leaving the village, and because, with three or four exceptions, none of her poetry was published until after her death, some of her early biographers represented Miss Dickinson as a recluse, a lonely spinster in a prison of her own making, spinning out her days in morbid, miserable longing.

As we have come more fully to know the poet and her poetry, however, we have realized how profoundly wrong that initial judgment was. For the truth is that Emily Dickinson was a woman who knew depths of joy and fulfillment as few people ever do. To live, she once said, is so startling that it leaves little room for other occupations. While most of her neighbors plodded along from day to day unaware of the glory shining from the

Holyoke Range or the pine-and-juniper beauty of the Pelham hills, Miss Dickinson drank in that glory, marveled at the wonder and meaning of it all, and, like another iconoclast down Concord way, traveled a good deal in Amherst.

One reason why Emily Dickinson may have confounded her biographers is that, more than most of us, she faced up to the essential solitariness of human life. Instinctively she understood this primal fact: that a human being must have the fortitude to live with himself or herself before he or she can live effectively with other people. She once wrote a poem in which she remarked that there are various kinds of solitude, but that the greatest of all is the solitude of the individual soul.

Before you and I can live with the world, we must be able amicably to live with ourselves. Put this down as one of the eternal verities. Miss Dickinson did, and understood and accepted it, and lived a rare, rich life in consequence. Oh, it's true, of course, that society crowds in upon us on every hand. All the time we are surrounded by people. We have our friends and loved ones and they mean the world to us. Yet in a very real existential sense we are alone, we feel and think alone, and, in the end, we die alone. Human life need not be lonely, but it must cope with this initial fact of aloneness. It must understand what Browning meant in asking, "When is a man strong until he feels alone?" Which is a way of saying that life is easy for us when we can rely on society, other people, someone else. But the really strong men and women are they who, in their solitariness, in their polar privacy, can still stand up to life and meet it undaunted.

We moderns have a good deal of trouble facing this truth because we are part of what David Riesman called **The Lonely Crowd.** By which he meant that most Americans today are outer rather than inner-directed people. We find much of our satisfaction in our symbiotic relationship as part of a group. We are organization men and women in more ways than simply being company employees. Too many of our ideas and values come from the group, mass media, pop culture. Without the womb-like protection of the group, we tend to feel lonely, insecure, frightened. We have no conception of what Swift meant when he said, "The wise man is never less alone than when he is alone."

If you and I are going to know one of the modern world's best-kept secrets, we will have to understand this cardinal truth. The message of real success in living is not the amount of money we have accumulated, or the fame we have achieved, or the knowledge we have acquired, or even the number of friends we have made. The measure ultimately is simply this: how well have we lived with ourselves? To unravel the secret, we must know ourselves . . . be ourselves . . . and quietly, serenely, harmoniously, live with ourselves.

"That, My Friends, is Character"

It is a warm Sunday morning in June 1865, only
two months after what may have been the most poig-
nant episode in American history: Lee's surrender to
Grant at Appomatox.

The scene is Richmond, Virginia, capitol of the
Confederacy, now occupied by Federal troops. Services
are being conducted as usual at historic St. Paul's
Episcopal Church. After the rector has completed his
sermon, he prepares to administer holy communion.

Suddenly the congregation is as shocked as though
cannon fire had broken out yet one more terrible time.
The unthinkable is happening. With dignity, a tall, well-
dressed black man is moving forward and advancing to
the communion table.

Members of the congregation who are about to rise
sink back stunned. Emancipation? Yes, it had to be expected. Defeat? Yes, tormentingly it has come. But
this! Quite unacceptable. No one stirs. The chancel rail
stands empty.

No one stirs, that is, except one man. Robert E.
Lee is sitting quietly in his familiar pew on the left side
aisle. Deliberately he rises and with his never-failing
composure slowly walks down the aisle. Now two men,
one black, one white, kneel at the chancel rail. Finally,
in a silence heavy with many meanings, other com-
municants come forward and bow their heads at St.
Paul's altar.

* * *

The principal difficulty in talking about character lies in trying to define it. One ends with an assortment of words, adequate in their way, perhaps, but without blood in their veins or breath in their being. They need to be animated, inspirited, exemplified. They need a tall gray man, brilliant in battle, indomitable in defeat, kind, wise, patient, beloved of his people as no one before or since him has been. They need such a man to breathe life into the words and to show the world what character really means.

Still, perhaps we can say this much about the matter. Character is the sum total of those qualities, especially of those moral qualities, that distinguish us as an individual, as a particular, unique human being. A person's character is the reality of himself, as opposed, for example, to his reputation, which is simply what other people think about him. Character is that incorruptible something that makes us dependable whether we are being watched or not, that makes us trustworthy and truthful, even when it would be to our advantage to be a little less than honest. As Macauley said, "The measure of a man's true character is what he would do if he knew he would never be found out." Character is what makes a man as chivalrous and greathearted in defeat as he would have been in victory. It is a sort of moral gyroscope within a person; it is a force that gives him the strength to do what he knows he ought to do; it is something above knowledge, intelligence, genius: it is, in fact, the governing element of the good man or woman's life.

To exemplify character, an illustrious host of men and women, some from the ranks of history, some from the common walks of everyday life, is available. Why Lee? Because he was one of our truly greatest countrymen, a man who, for reasons perhaps inevitable, has not yet received his due. Because in war, in peace, in all ways, he was a magnificent embodiment of what we mean by the difficult-to-define quality we have been talking about here.

* * *

Let us return to that Virginia church and see again what is happening there. Robert E. Lee has just lost a war, but as he kneels at St. Paul's altar, he may be winning something even greater . . .

That, my friends, is character.

Which Kind of Person Are You?

Hippocrates, the ancient Greek physician, is justly celebrated as the father of medicine because he was the first man to place the healing profession on something like a scientific basis. He also seems to have been a sort of aboriginal psychologist for he divided human beings into four primary groups on the basis of temperament. There are, said he, phlegmatic, or sluggish and apathetic people; sanguine, or happy and cheerful people; choleric, or angry and hot-tempered people; and melancholy, or sad and gloomy people. Although it was formulated almost twenty-five centuries ago, this quadruple division still makes an abundance of sense and suggests a good deal that is revealing about you, me and that confusing neighbor next door.

For instance, let's suppose you are one of those phlegmatic persons who travels slowly and quietly through life, seldom getting out of third gear. You never make much of a splash; you favor rockers over rockets; you just do your everyday job and you carry your own little load.

Well, hear this: you are one of the people society could not do without. You may not be the most vivacious girl in the office or the most popular fellow in the shop, yet much of the world's daily work is done by men and women like you. By your very weight, by your solidity and dependability, you help keep the world swinging steady on its course. The rest of us owe you more than you, or we, know.

Now let's suppose you are that second type, one of those perennially merry, joyful, upbeat people who habitually assume that the sun will always shine on their picnic, and that that, indeed, is what life blissfully is. As you romp through the years, you exert a contagious and buoyant effect on the rest of us. There is something about your unquenchable cheerfulness and confidence that carries over and helps lift us to sunnier heights than we might otherwise know. Bless you for being what you so radiantly are.

Then there is the choleric person, the human firecracker, who doesn't even need matches to blow himself up. He is someone we walk around warily, like a rumbling volcano. His anger may erupt at any time and its heat can singe and burn. His name may be Thomas Carlyle, about whom someone said that he had a daily secretion of curses he had to vent on something or somebody.

Yet here again, tempestuous though he may be, is a personality type our equivocal old world sorely needs. His effusions or explosions clear away a lot of the sham and hypocrisy of life. Sometimes he gets so mad that he just bursts right out and tells the truth, and damn the consequences. Whoever called the prophets of ancient Israel "God's angry men" was an appreciative judge of choleric character.

Or let's suppose we have to do with one of those melancholy types who lives over on the shadowy side of the street where the sun doesn't shine very much. The sorrow and sadness of the world weigh heavily upon him and life often seems a gloomy business, "a walking shadow," in Shakespeare's words.

Surely the foremost example in American history of this kind of temperament was Abraham Lincoln, a frequently and, at times, almost dangerously melancholy man. More than once he contemplated suicide and on several occasions friends felt it necessary to remove knives and other potentially dangerous weapons from his reach. He laughed often, but, as he confessed, he laughed to keep from crying.

If only the Jeremiahs and Schopenhauers and Lincolns of this world could understand how inestimably much they give the rest of us, their "encircling gloom" might be lightened considerably. For they go down to the depths and they find strange dark treasures there, truths that have to be learned in the murk of sorrow, pain and despair, and they bring them back for the edification and salvation of the rest of us. They help us understand much about the deeper meanings and higher values of life we might never otherwise know.

The point of it all is that no matter which kind of person we tend to be — and certainly it is unnecessary to say that none of us is wholly any one type, most of us are admixtures of all four, with one likely dominant — each of us has something **sui generis,** of unique value to give the world. Because each type of temperament reveals some aspect of human experience which is hidden to the others and we need them all that the human portrait may be fully fleshed out.

So remember that whichever you tend to be — phlegmatic, cheerful, stormy or melancholy — you are part of the marvelous mosaic of human life and without YOU the picture would not be complete.

Frankie's Monsters

Until he died two years ago at the ripe old canine age of 17, my wife and I had a miniature poodle named Frankie who was as delightful as only dogs (and maybe dolphins) can be. Frankie had a genuine sense of humor, a wonderful sense of play, a great deal of affection and an enviable ability to get what he wanted.

But like all God's creatures, even Frankie was not quite perfect. I regret to report that Monsieur Francois was more than a little neurotic. He was frequently troubled by an assortment of monsters, and the one thing they all had in common — this, by the way, is a characteristic of monsters — is that they didn't really exist, except in Frankie's perfervid imagination.

Let me introduce you to a couple of those chimeras. We met one several summers ago when we stopped overnight at a country motel. Outside that hostelry was what seemed, at least to Frankie, to be a r-e-a-l l-i-v-e MONSTER! It had one flashing green eye and one great glaring, flaring red eye and it constantly spurted water from its huge menacing mouth. Actually, the thing was nothing but a fountain illuminated at night by a green and red light. But from the way Frankie acted and reacted, you can bet your bottom dollar **he** thought it was a monster and he wasn't taking any chances.

Then at our summer home in Maine there is the Wind Monster. Situated as we are on a little peninsula with water on three sides, we have a good deal of wind which often makes strange, spooky, spectral noises. Frankie never completely accepted the wind, but sometimes jumped and growled as though lions and tigers were prowling just outside his door. There were also the Floor Furnace Monster and the Cuisinart Monster and the Washing Machine Monster, and a lot of other demons I could tell you about.

But enough of Frankie's Minotaurs. You and I have so many of our own that I expect we had better spend the rest of our space talking about them. I may have begun these remarks facetiously, but there is really nothing funny at all about the monster menace problem that troubles each of us. Like poor old Frankie, every one of us has certain fears, phobias, fantasies, silly things he or she is afraid of, that may well be called monsters. And again, as in Frankie's case, most of them are imaginary; they are not fact, but fiction; they prowl only through the Stygian caves of our own hallucinating minds.

Somewhere I have read a story about a medical research scientist who kept a collection of jars in his laboratory containing the enlarged hearts of more than a score of people. To visitors, he frequently said, "All these men and women died of the same disease." Naturally the visitors asked, "What was it?" And the scientist would reply, "The disease called fear."

In every instance, case studies had indicated no physical, but only functional, or non-organic, reasons for the person's death. Compulsive worry, anxiety, tension, stress and strain had apparently done them all in. It would not be scientific, and one could scarcely put this down as "cause of death" on a medical certificate, but it might well be accurate to say that they died of — fear.

The pitiful absurdity involved here is that so often the fears that kill us, like Frankie's monsters, are fanciful, not factual. They are hobgoblins of the spirit. They are monsters of the mind. They are demons from unconscious depths. This is certainly not to say that there isn't an intimidating assortment of problems and perils in this world about which you and I should be gravely (sic) concerned. Indeed, there is a frightening battery of threats and menaces by which we ought to be scared (almost) to death.

But we are talking here about imaginary monsters, about fears that don't really come true. Veterans in the mental health field never stop shaking their heads over one of the most common and foolish of ironies: that we humans worry ourselves sick about things that seldom, if ever, happen, yet we are blithely unconcerned about the terribly real and serious dangers that threaten our very existence.

By all and every means, be afraid of the dreadful things that war and hate and selfishness and prejudice can do. Fear for the future as you fear for your life since your life will depend on how we handle our nuclear tomorrows. But don't be afraid of monsters-in-motels, and things that **don't** go bump in the night, and wind in spruce boughs, and all the other silly spooks that frightened poor old Frankie. Fear the truly monstrous things in this world and fight against them mightily. But don't let yourself be frightened by — Frankie's monsters.

The Most Commonly Overlooked Secret of Happiness

The "secret" I have in mind here is so seemingly simple I hesitated for awhile before venturing to speak of it. But it is a secret that could make an eye-and-mind-opening difference in all our lives. Moreover, because of its very simplicity it is one of those truths we are likely to overlook in the hurry and scurry of modern life. So here it is, one secret I am delighted to give away!

Actually, it is nothing more or less than the homely fact that most of us do not make as much of an effort as we should consciously to relish and appreciate life. For that unpretentious reason we miss in our living much of the joy and happiness, the richness and fullness that ought to be ours. The key word here — the heart of the secret — is the word **appreciate** or **appreciation.**

All around us everywhere is a world bursting with the beauty of sight, sound, odor and sensory feeling. Yet because we fail to make a more conscious effort at enjoyment and appreciation, we go our insensate ways like all the rest of the twentieth century machines. "Life has loveliness to sell," to give away; the gods have been profligate with beauty, flinging it into every wayside puddle and carpeting the earth with it as with flowers in May. Furthermore, there are few days in our lives, even the dark and dreary ones, when at least a few shining moments do not transform the gloom.

Joshua Loth Liebman began his enormously

popular book of a few decades ago by telling about an old rabbi who once advised him that the most precious boon one could wish for is peace of mind. Not far down on that same list should be "the power of expecting happiness from common things." This is akin to the sentiment of an English writer who said the four nicest things are tea, a fire, a book and a friend. To which a compatriot added one more item: a mind that can see so much in such simple things.

In one of his essays, the sixteenth century French writer Montaigne says he realizes only too well how short this life of ours is, and therefore by the zest of his enjoyment he will make up for life's hasty ebbing. "The shorter my possession of life, the fuller and deeper must I live it."

True enough, any thinking person would agree. Well, agree we may, yet how many of us make Montaigne's effort consciously to savor and enjoy life to the full? I fear that too often I for one do not. Sometimes an entire day goes by when I forget to enjoy, when I make no attempt to appreciate an abundance of little things: the good taste of my food; that glowing, vibrant feeling my body has after a vigorous walk; the aerial fairyland of cloud formations above my head; a witty quip overheard in the street; the unexpected kindness of a stranger. Because I have made no conscious effort to appreciate these modest pleasures of body, mind and spirit, I have simply existed during this particular day, not especially unhappy, perhaps, but not perceptively happy either, just an automaton mechanically doing my work.

Too bad I haven't recalled that old Chinese proverb that rings with such a common sense sound: "En-joy yourself; it is later than you think." This is a summary way of saying that since ours is the only world we know, we had better make the most of it while we are still here. Tomorrow may be too late. Let's make of life a friendly, warm, winsome affair, pressing the last morsel of flavor from it. Then when death raps quietly at our garden gate, we will be able to go away with him, contented and at peace with our living.

To the man or woman who enjoys the mystery of the commonplace and the beauty of the ordinary, happiness is rarely absent for he or she lives surrounded by the raw material of which happiness is made. Here is one person who has **not** failed to learn and to live by what I have chosen to call the most commonly overlooked secret of happiness.

What Security Really Is

Back in the summer of 1956, a college alumnus friend of mine, Bob Manry, did what seemed to most people like an utterly foolhardy thing. All by himself he sailed across the Atlantic Ocean in a 13½ foot boat, the Tinkerbelle. It took him more than two months, but, so help me, somehow or other he made it.

I have seen and examined Tinkerbelle and, frankly, I don't think I would have had the nerve to sail that thing across the Hudson River. But Bob Manry had. Why? Because he had something that is worth more than all the money in all of Switzerland's vaults. Bob had security, a deep-running, undergirdling confidence that nothing seemed able to break.

More specifically, what he had was an unshakable faith in himself, in the strength, skill and knowledge he knew were inside of him. And he had an equal faith in the sea, in the world outside of him. Bob was sure that if he played the game according to the rules of the sea, if he cooperated with the titanic forces of nature, he would be able to sail that tiny cockleshell across 3000 miles of Atlantic Ocean. And, by the great beard of Neptune, he did!

What it all added up to was a kind of confidence and self-reliance, a triumphant faith in himself and in certain factors and forces outside of himself that in the end meant that most sustaining of qualities — security.

Too many people here in our day are misled by an

unfortunate and unrealistic notion that security is something that can somehow be guaranteed, whether by the government, or society, or a pension policy, or whatever. Yet beyond a limited material point, that simply isn't true. Basically, life is an insecure business. It always has been and, indubitably, it always will be.

By this I mean that nothing can really protect you and your loved ones against defeat, depression, despair, disgrace, disaster and death itself. Calamity can occur at any time — and it frequently does. There is no positive assurance that you and I will not be dead before another day has passed. The adult who tries to build physical or material walls against adversity is like a child on the seashore who tries to build a wall of sand against the incoming tide.

What we have to understand is that security is much more closely related to the inward strength, sureness and values a man or woman has than it is to any outward circumstance. Your really secure person is the individual who has discovered that he has within himself the resolution and the resources to take whatever life may throw against him.

Oh, he knows he isn't Superman. He knows each of us has his breaking point. But he also knows that, come hell or high water, come defeat and disgrace, come death and disaster, somehow or other he **is** going to pull through. He knows this because he has discovered powers and potentials inside of him that support him. And he has found ideas, ideals and values outside of him that support him. And between them, those inner and outer forces give him enough strength to see it through, whatever "it" may be.

People often wonder about men like Bob Manry. About the men and women who climb "unclimbable" mountains, cross the Sahara alone, fight their way through Amazon jungles or sail solo around the world. It's not only a question of why they do it, but of how they do it. What force keeps them going, sustains them, drives them on?

I think we would all agree that such men and women must possess a remarkable combination of qualities, including strength, courage and sheer, dogged determination. But high on that list has to be the indispensable quality of security.

Abounding evidence indicates that the people who get more out of life are so often the same people who have found in life the stalwart, sustaining quality Bob Manry had. Why, it even carried him in a 13½ foot boat all the way across the Atlantic Ocean!

On Making Our Dreams Come True

It was the sort of day, dark, gloomy, overcast, that people associate with funerals. I stood before an open grave, and as I listened to the familiar words of the committal service, a thought kept troubling my mind. Because, you see, I had known this man well. He had had the usual complement of hopes and dreams, but when he died at the age of only 58 most of those dreams had died with him — they had never come true.

I do not mean to say that his life had been a failure. On the contrary, it had been a good, decent, compassionate life. But in terms of the realization of many of his dearest dreams, it had not been a success either.

I have often wondered, frequently on such occasions as I have just described, how common his story is. Too common, I'm afraid. The mournful fact is that while many of us have dreams of what we would like to do with our lives, of goals we would like to achieve, so often nothing much comes of those dreams. Slowly they fade with the passing years, leaving only a wistful longing for a splendor that might have been.

Because they know I love the scene it portrays, several years ago some friends gave me a jigsaw puzzle. When put together, as I can tell from the photo on the cover of the box, it composes a captivating picture of New Harbor, one of my favorite New England fishing villages. The only trouble is, I have never taken the time to assemble the pieces. Thus I have never had the satisfaction of seeing that picture take shape before my eyes and become a reality.

Like me and my puzzle, so many of us have never taken the time to put the pieces of our dream together. So it stays in its box, unformed and covered with dust. Of all the epitaphs I have run across, the saddest may be the salesman, Willie Loman's, "He never really lived." People who do not at least try to realize their dreams seldom live life as fully and satisfyingly as they could and should.

Before we can do that, however, we have to have some sense of what our dream is, of where we want to go and how and why. But you may object, doesn't everybody know what he wants? Don't we all have a radiant mental image of what we want our dream castle to be like?

The answer is a sharp and stinging no. You and I would be surprised if only we could know how many of us have no clear or reasonable idea of what we really want to do with our lives. The trouble is that in our younger days it's difficult to answer this question because we have not had sufficient experience with life and the world.

Then we get started down a particular path — although "rut" might be a more appropriate word for it — and after awhile we find, or at least we feel, ourselves trapped in that rut. The effort to break out seems more than we care to make. So we move in whatever direction the rut takes us and not down our own "yellow brick road" to Wonderland.

Think of a random assortment of people you know and see if you do not agree with me. We move, and we move rapidly these days, but not toward any well-chosen goal. More often we are like a doe I once saw caught in a savage current. The doe was going where the current carried it, not where it wanted to go.

Happiness comes about in assorted ways. The wrong way is by a road called Detour; the right way by a road called Decision. As wisely and well as we can, we have to decide what it is that we really want out of life, where we truly want to go, and then by an effort of will, we have to point our life in that direction. The English poet Henley may have been a bit over-confident when he defiantly declared, "I am the master of my fate." Still, that sort of self-assurance is likely to carry a man a lot farther toward the castle of his dreams than the fellow who confuses drifting and dreaming.

Martin Luther King, Jr. once said, "In order to be a dreamer, you have to have a dream." May you too have your dreams . . . may they be worthy ones . . . and may you have the will and the vision to make them come true.

What Courage Really Is

Years ago when I was a cub reporter on the old **Detroit Times**, I had the privilege of interviewing Amelia Earhart. She had been the first woman to cross the Atlantic in an airplane and the first woman to fly the Atlantic alone. She was America's first-lady-of-the-air and in the hour or so I talked with her, I could well understand why.

There are some people who impress us just by being what they essentially are. It isn't anything they say; it is a kind of strength or power that emanates from them. That's the way it was with Amelia Earhart. There was a quiet sense of control and confidence about her that was as real and tangible as the paper on which I wrote my notes. If I hadn't known, I think I would have felt that here was a woman who was giving to, and getting a lot more out of, life than most of us do. Somehow, I realized, she knew the secret.

About a year after that interview, while she was attempting a flight around the world, Amelia Earhart was lost. Presumably her plane went down somewhere in mid-Pacific. At any rate, she was never heard from again.

As long as I live, I will never forget how stunned I was as I stared at the headline that told the tragic news. And there is something else I will never forget. In those first few desolating moments, I had the most vivid impression of an airplane going down and down into the interminable reaches of the far Pacific and of a woman calmly facing her destiny and paying in the noble coin of courage for it.

Because I remembered a poem Miss Earhart had written called "Courage" and one line in it especially: "Courage is the price that life exacts for granting peace." It was her way of saying that you and I can get what we want out of life, all right, but we have to pay the price. And a sizeable part of the price is courage.

Moreover, she was one person who knew what courage really is. As she realized full well, it is a good deal more than sheer recklessness. Those history-making flights of hers were planned as cautiously and carefully as a military campaign. Sometimes we do have to take chances, as of course she did, but they ought to be risks taken in behalf of wise and worthwhile ends.

Here is something else she knew: that one can be courageous and still be afraid. Anybody who doesn't feel fear when the bombs fall or the hurricane strikes or the plane goes down is not courageous, he or she is just plain crazy! Courage is not the absence of fear. It is the capacity to do what has to be done even though our knees are shaking and our nerves are shrieking. Never apologize for being afraid. Only be concerned that you may not handle fear in the right way. As somebody has written, "Courage is fear that has said its prayers."

And Amelia Earhart also knew — she said this on a number of occasions — that courage is not the special province or possession of a few privileged people whom we call heroes. Studies made of the matter suggest most people worry that they may not measure up when the big challenges come and their mettle is really put to the test. Well, stop worrying. Those same studies — not to mention personal experiences many of us have had — indicate that so-called average people have plenty of the special strength called courage. They also reveal that when it is needed that emergency power is instinctively released. We don't deliberately decide to act courageously. We just do. It is almost like the adrenalin in our bodies, a glandular "shot-in-the-arm" that automatically comes to the rescue when we need it most.

It has been a good many years now since Amelia Earhart's plane disappeared in the Pacific's vastness and she paid the ultimate price. But from everything we know about her we have to believe she found it richly worth the paying. Despite the passing of the years and the waning of many memories, I have never forgotten the unspoken lesson I learned from her that winter night in Detroit.

If you want to share it with me, always remember these words of America's greatest woman flier, "Courage is the price that life exacts for granting peace."

Survival Lesson

How is such a thing possible? Out on the desolate windswept Maine coast island it clung to the barren rock like the last lone hope of the world. The little tree — it was a spruce — grew out of a crack in the rock scarcely wider than a twig is wide. Seemingly, its roots went down into granite. There was no soil apparent and, given the angle of the crack, rain water must have run off as soon as it fell. Summer and winter savage easterly winds tore at the tree and sometimes when the tide was high, great waves crashed against it.

Still, the tree survived. There was no other living thing — no blade of grass, or root of hemlock, or laurel or alder or pine — only that little tree, alone, enduring not so much by a miracle as by something else . . .

One does not speak of stamina, courage and will where a tree is concerned. But one can see a tree as a symbol of such virtues. And if one can learn much about stamina, courage and will from the heroes and supermen and women of the race, he can also learn more than a little from a lonely spruce, wind-torn and storm-tossed, growing only God knows how and surviving by a force stronger than the rock beneath it.

* * * * * * * * * * *

From Maine to Arizona is a long way by car — and an even longer way, geologically and botanically speaking. But the road leads at last to another part of our country any hardy soul is likely to fall in love with. The Sonoran desert. Here the waves are sand, not sea, yet they roll like ocean swells across the southern half of Arizona and part of northern Mexico. Unlike the Mojave or the Sahara, however, which are really dead deserts, the Sonoran is a living desert. Only you would never know this from casually looking at it. Actually, that arid reach has a startling variety of growth flowering almost everywhere, but you are not apt to notice it at first glance because much of it is desert or earth-colored. What you have to do is take a horse and ride off in any direction — there aren't many fences on the Sonoran desert — and keep your eyes open, and soon you will see 20 or 30 different kinds of cactus and ocotillo and little paloverde trees and a spiky variety of other flora and fauna.

That desert is simply alive with growing things, and for a few weeks in the spring of the year when those plants blossom in brilliant reds and yellows and purples, the Sonoran desert is one of the most unforgettable sights you are likely to see on the planet Earth.

Now here is another believe-it-or-not fact about the Sonoran: it averages only five or six inches of rain **a year**! Back on the Atlantic coast, though a long way south of Maine, the Florida peninsula sometimes gets that much rain in a single day. The startling aridity of the desert means that to exist its vegetation has had to develop some exceedingly ingenious and unlikely ways of storing up water. For months on end it receives no rain at all; the hot sun beats down day after merciless day; there is no shade; and then because there is so little moisture in the ground and atmosphere, the nights may be surprisingly cold. One wonders how in the world any vegetation manages to survive.

And yet survive it does! — that's the point. The cacti and all the other flora of the Sonoran desert and the spruce and birch and hemlock seemingly growing right out of the granite ledges of coastal Maine, somehow they do survive. Apparently there is a force that enables them, by whatever adaptive and sometimes fantastic processes, to endure. In some wondrous way it does keep life going, even under circumstances where you wouldn't think life had a ghost of a chance. With William James and Bernard Shaw and Albert Schweitzer, many of us choose to call that something "life force" because this is the simplest and most accurate way to describe what we mean.

And I can testify that standing out on the granite shelves of Harbor Island facing the Gulf of Maine and looking at a little spruce growing where nothing, much less a tree, should be able to grow, is a profoundly strengthening and sustaining experience. After all, there are times when the problem is not how to get more out of life. The problem is simply how to keep life going. I'm afraid I do not know the answer to this ageless enigma, but I have a feeling in my bones that somehow a little spruce tree may . . .

The Advantages of
Being an Optimist

One of the suspect words in the American vocabulary, as far as a good many academicians and intellectuals are concerned, is a term they equate with a shallow, sentimental attitude toward life. Which is a bit odd if you know its antecedents for it is descended from the Latin **optimus** meaning "the best." They put a kind of reserve English on it, however, and end up with something like "banal," "saccharine," "superficial." In all fairness, one has to admit that a recent spate of happiness-through-cheerfulness books plus a good deal of Pollyanna preachment has not helped poor optimism's image any.

But let us not be put off by a disdain the word has only occasionally deserved. Optimism as a belief in the essential goodness of the universe is scarcely puerile stuff. It has a whole serious other side suggested by these words of William James, a man who was likely this country's most eminent psychologist-philosopher: "Be not afraid of life. Believe that life **is** worth living, and your belief will help create the fact." From somber experience, James knew what he was talking about, for after passing through his own dark valley, he emerged into the sunlight, and for the rest of his days unabashedly proclaimed a buoyantly optimistic philosophy of life.

First of all, he advised us, such an attitude results in definite physical advantages. A physician as well as a pundit, he knew the clinical evidence is overwhelming that people who are consistently cheerful, hopeful, optimistic are less subject to many kinds of illnesses than their gloomy, depressive friends. He was not jesting when he said, "The Lord may forgive us our sins, but the nervous system never does." Or as another M.D., speaking in the same vein, declared, "You do not get stomach ulcers from what you eat; you get ulcers from what is eating you."

No, there is abundant evidence that genuine optimism brings us rewards in the form of both physical and psychical well-being that we still do not sufficiently appreciate, even in this progressive era of psychosomatic medicine.

But the values of optimism are not only personal, they have some dynamic social implications as well. For the pleasant fact is that the consistently optimistic individual is likely to be more of a success socially, that is, in his relations with other people, and to that extent he is a happier and a better adjusted person. Joseph Addison suggested that "cheerfulness is a kind of daylight in the mind." Not only does that inner light irradiate your own inner life, but it shines out through your eyes and words and whole personality and attracts other people to it.

Or to change the metaphor a bit, may we not say that cheerfulness is a magnet and that it functions as a magnet does. Which accounts for the attraction it exerts and why we respond so readily to the truly optimistic individual. Something of his light and liveliness are conveyed to us by the electromagnetic force of the positive personality, and our own lives are brightened and reinforced accordingly. Scores of people who had the privilege of associating in any way with Franklin Roosevelt have testified that it was not so much what the man said or did as what he so radiantly was that charged their spirits and bolstered their faith. The optimism — that's the only word for it — of the man was so vibrant and energizing that it infused an entire nation with renewed vigor and hope.

Something of the same sort can be said for Roosevelt's great good friend and co-leader of the free world, Winston Churchill. Perhaps Sir Winston's driving force was not so much optimism as it is popularly understood as a bulldog conviction and invincible will. But however you define it, it was a dynamic that, perhaps more than any other single factor, carried Britain through its darkest hours and on to what had seemed an impossible victory. "Death and sorrow will be the companions of our journey; hardship our garment; constancy and valor our only shield. We must be united, we must be undaunted, we must be inflexible." That is not precisely what we think of as optimistic talk, yet in spirit and conviction it triumphantly was.

Optimism as a facile philosophy of self-delusion and wishful thinking? As an "every day in every way I'm getting better and better" quick-fix nostrum? What egregious nonsense! Genuine, finely tempered optimism is the conviction that life is essentially good, that mankind can prevail, and that the future, however perilous the prospect, may still see the fulfillment of our dreams and the vindication of our faith.

The Varieties of Love

More than most people, we Americans tend to be inveterate romantics. So perhaps it is understandable that we should tend to think of love in excessively romantic terms. Love to us is a valentine, heart-shaped and sugar sweet. It is bluebirds and orange blossoms and stardust and moonlight. It's "John loves Mary" carved on an old oak tree.

And that's wonderful! There's nothing in the world wrong with romantic love. If it doesn't make the world go round, it certainly makes it go more merrily. Still, maybe we ought to take time out occasionally and consider this fact: when psychology talks about love, it is likely to think of the matter in four quite different ways.

At the very beginning of the human story, with the newborn baby, the psychologist is concerned about love. Devoutly, he hopes it will be a love story. Because he knows — repeatedly, clinical experience has demonstrated the fact — that that tiny infant wants and needs affection and is almost certain to suffer without it.

In fact, without it his whole future may be affected. Suddenly and painfully ejected from his mother's womb, that helpless creature needs the reassurances of affection almost as much as he needs milk to nourish his body.

Then as the baby grows into childhood and adolescence, his need for love assumes a different form. Of all the stages of human growth, in many respects adolescence is the most difficult. Now what this young person needs, particularly from his parents and those around him, is a different kind of love. It is the kind that gives him understanding and support as he struggles with the confusing process of trying to become an adult. It is the kind of love that says, I remember what you're going through, and I know it's tough, and I just want you to realize that I understand.

Finally our young friend makes it. He does grow into adulthood. Soon love with him assumes still a different form. He meets a woman, or she meets a man, and in that other person much of the meaning of his or her life is bound up. Now love becomes not so much a matter of receiving, which is what it has been pretty largely to date, but rather a matter of giving. Now he learns what is perhaps the most beatific of human secrets: that when he gives his love fully and freely, he gets back love fully and freely. This is the wonderful human paradox: what he wants in life, he gets by giving. And love is the magic catalyst that does the trick.

Then, at last, inevitably, the twilight years come on. Perhaps his wife has already died. His children have long ago left home. Most of his friends are gone. The lights are fading out one by one. Now he stands in need of a final kind of love. It is the kind that tells him that he is still wanted and needed, that makes him feel there is still meaning to life and a real place in the world for him.

Here in our day millions of men and women are living to a considerably older age than most people reached in the past. Which means there are innumerable human beings all around us who deeply need this fourth variety of love. The most destructive experience of old age is loneliness. And the gentlest antidote for loneliness is caring, sharing and loving.

All of these are reasons why both ancient philosophers and modern psychologists have put love at the head of the list of human needs and virtues. Just as the body must have food, water and air to sustain it, so the spirit must have love if life is not to be a barren and stunted passage. Love is not only a June-moon-spoon affair, delightful as that may be. At every phase of human life, it is a psychological and spiritual necessity.

This is why, in order to get what we want to get, and ought to get, out of life, you and I must learn how to give and receive love. And of the two, the giving is the greater. When we are able to give our love fully and freely, we needn't concern ourselves any longer with this persisting question of how to get more out of life. Because more will come, richer and in greater abundance than ever we dreamed.

The View From The
Top of The Hill

One of my present-day heroes — I wish there were more of them — was Adlai Stevenson. I do not know when we have had as urbane, sensitive, civilized a man in public affairs, and I devoutly wish his tribe would increase. We were fortunate that two such exceptional candidates as Adlai Stevenson and Dwight Eisenhower ran for the Presidency at the same time. We were unfortunate that both of them could not have had the opportunity of serving that office.

When Adlai Stevenson was governor of Illinois, 1948-52, occasionally he liked to escape to a country hilltop not far from the capitol in Springfield and stand there and look out over long vistas of Midwestern fields. He said a man couldn't get a more intense feeling for America than he could from that hilltop. He also said that when Abraham Lincoln was in Springfield he did the same thing: he would come out to that rise of prairie land like a man hurrying to an oasis, and there, for a little while at least, he would find surcease from the problems that plagued him. It was such a noble precedent and, apparently, such a restorative experience, that Governor Stevenson would sometimes remain for hours on end.

A person does not need to be much of a seer to know why those two great men went there and what they found there. In one word: perspective. Your dictionary will tell you that perspective is the ability to see all relevant details in a meaningful relationship. But I think the Lincoln-Stevenson story tells it better. What both of them must have found was a clarification of vision. Standing there on that height in the wind and the sun, they must have been able to see the perplexing, burdensome details of their duties "in a meaningful relationship."

Obviously, a man can see farther from the top of a hill than he can from the bottom. What perspective does is take us to the top of the hill and show us the world, not as it confusedly seems, but as it actually is. It separates the trees so we can see the forest. It helps us make sense out of nonsense and fact out of fancy.

So does perspective in another field: that of art. Here it is a matter of representing three-dimensional space on a flat surface like a painting or in certain kinds of bas-relief sculpture. It is a technique which makes painted objects seem more realistic by establishing their relative dimensions, or their "meaningful relationships," and by variations in color, contour and light and dark. During the past five hundred years it has done wonders for painters and their painting. The magic of perspective has made the world as the artist offers it to us look like the world as we actually see it.

When I think of perspective and its meaning for our lives, I vividly remember the first time I climbed a promontory a little more dramatic than Lincoln and Stevenson's knoll. The most magnificient view on this country's entire Atlantic coast is to be seen from the top of Mt. Cadillac on the island of Mount Desert on the shores of Maine. Mount Desert has often been called America's most beautiful island, and it may well be so. Certainly the view from the top of Cadillac is unsurpassed on all the Eastern seaboard.

As one drives up Maine's rugged and ragged shoreline, he is hopelessly confused by the profusion of bays, coves, inlets and islands, and he learns to appreciate the fact that while the state's coast is 300 miles long as the sea gull flies, it is 3000 miles long as the fish swims, or by water.

And yet when he comes to Mount Desert and climbs to the top of Cadillac, his confusion is dispelled as though by a miracle, and bays, coves and islands arrange themselves before his eyes. Here is the world as it actually is and not as his mixed-up mind fallibly envisioned it.

It seems to me that this is what perspective does for a person: It takes him up to the top of the range and shows him the world, not as the crazy kaleidoscope it sometimes seems, but as a related, integrated, harmonious whole. It shows him life as an ever-growing process, humanity as a brother-and-sisterhood, and the universe as the unity its name says it is.

To get more out of life and to know the world as it really is, one must climb to a goodly height and see them steadily and see them whole.

Making Every Day Thanksgiving Day

Once upon a rugged time I spent a whole summer traveling in Asia, often in the more remote and backward areas of that part of the world. When an American travels as I did, eating the sort of food and drinking the water he finds there, he is likely to become sick. As a matter of fact, I do not see how he can help it.

Woefully, that was what happened to me. I was somewhere in India; to this day I have no idea where. One dispiriting night I found myself in a ramshackle old inn that was straight out of Rudyard Kipling. Sometime during those interminable hours I got up, stumbled to a window and stood there for a long time looking out into the strange Indian darkness.

I was sick that night in three ways. I was certainly sick of body. I was a little sick of mind. By this I mean I was unhappy and depressed. And I was assuredly sick of heart and spirit. Any American who can travel through India and not be sick of spirit at the poverty, misery and suffering he finds so widely spread — well, such a person has to be more insensitive than I am.

Standing there in the palpable darkness of the Indian night, I made a promise to myself. I said, When I get back to my own country, without making a nuisance of myself, I am going to remind my fellow countrymen of something they too often forget, and that is how immeasurably much we have to be thankful for.

What is more I have kept that promise through the years, just as I am doing now. In scores of sermons, lecture platform appearances and broadcasts, I have made it a point to remind my audiences of how fantastically generous the fates have been to us. I have said, "For you, Thanksgiving may come on the fourth Thursday of November. But for me, after some of the desolating experiences I have had, every day here in America is Thanksgiving Day."

A little mawkish and chauvinistic? I think not. Not after that lost-in-India night when I learned the threefold nature of sickness. When I speak of the multitudinous things we Americans have to be thankful for, I am not speaking now of all our precious freedoms, rights and opportunities. After all, these are the verities that make our country truly great. But more of them later on.

I am speaking here of things as elementary as a glass of water. There have been times in the back country of Asia when I would gladly have paid 20 dollars for a glass of the sort of water that is available from almost any water tap here in America. I am speaking of the fact that you and I can walk into any supermarket or, with few exceptions, any restaurant and be sure the food we get is safe and edible. I am speaking of the roofs most of us have over our heads and of the clothes we have on our backs. Things as simple as these.

Of course poverty remains a serious, indeed critical, problem here in our country. Still, people are not dying by the dozens on our streets every night as I have seem them die on the sidewalks of Calcutta. And I have seen sights almost as heartrending in Egypt and the Middle East, in the slums of Naples, in Haiti, and in the barrios of South America.

This is what I mean when I speak of the simple, elementary things of life we Americans take so casually for granted. Like everything else, poverty and privation are relative matters. Clearly they are disgraceful afflictions in this country too, and clearly we must do everything we can to eliminate them. I am simply saying that in other parts of the world they are considerably worse.

Further, I am saying that those of us who are reasonably well off, who have enough food, clothing and housing for ourselves and our families and friends, are more fortunate than we ever know. Finally, I am saying that the getting more out of life is far easier for us than it is for them.

This is why I invite you to join me in an everyday celebration of Thanksgiving Day. If you do, it will help me keep a promise I once made to myself . . .

"He Grew Into Greatness"

More books have been written about Abraham Lincoln, it seems safe to say, than about any other American. And no wonder. For beneath the red-white-and-blue bunting in which we have draped him, beyond all the legends and the patriotic rhetoric and the Great Emancipator statuary, is an enigma and a mystery. The puzzle can be put plainly enough in six words: Where did Abraham Lincoln come from?

All romanticizing aside, the blunt fact seems to be that as a young man he was not a particularly remarkable person. If you had met him as he drifted down the Mississippi on a raft, or was running the post office at New Salem, or was serving in the state legislature of Illinois, I do not think you would have been uncommonly impressed.

It is true he came of good, husky, working folk stock; some of his forebears had fought laudably in the Revolutionary War; but as far as heredity was concerned there was little to suggest that Lincoln would be little more than a sturdy, capable pioneer-farmer.

And as for environmental influence, we all know what that was like. Born in a log cabin in the Kentucky wilderness, Abe did not go to school more than a single year in his life. What he knew best was hardship. There was a winter in Indiana when the Lincoln family was obliged to live in a tiny lean-to, one side of which was open to the weather.

It is sometimes contended that the harsh adversity he knew so well, the grinding poverty, the struggle to gain any sort of education strengthened the fiber of the man and made him what he so staunchly became. The rebuttal, of course, is that many thousands of other young men lived under conditions almost as trying; and yet in their case environment worked no such trans- forming wonders.

So — back to our initial question: Where did Abe Lincoln come from? How can we explain the mystery the man poses?

Let me suggest an answer. Abraham Lincoln had an aptitude amounting to genius for learning from ex- perience. For so many of us, hardship, sorrow, suffer- ing, disappointment are simply misfortunes, period. We may endure them because we have to, but how much do we learn from them? Here was a man, however, for whom these trials and testings were raw material for the creation of character. It is a well-worn cliche to say that the same fire that destroys the wood hardens the steel. But in Lincoln's case the platitude turns out to be a living reality. The man became great, or, more ac- curately, he grew into greatness as the fires of disap- pointment and adversity strengthened rather than destroyed him.

Out of many available, consider just two examples of that growth. In his earlier years, Abe was no more patient and forbearing than the next young fellow. In fact, on one occasion his intemperance caused him to be challenged to a duel which providentially was called off only at the last minute.

But oh how the patience of the man grew with the ongoing years. For decades the threat of civil war had hung darkly over the land. When war finally came, it seemed interminable. The maddening incompetence of the Union generals, at least until Lincoln found Grant; the hideous slaughter whose magnitude no one had anticipated; the constant conniving and the deception on the part of his own cabinet ministers and counselors; only a man with the patience of Job could have endured what Lincoln did.

Or consider this dimension of his growth. Lincoln's feeling for people, his ever-increasing sensitivity and greatness of heart, his never-failing compassion for the South and its suffering too: these are qualities we all now venerate as we might a saint's.

But the younger Lincoln, he of the scathing satire, of the anonymous letters, of the crude, sometimes cruel, frontier humor had a deal to learn about pity and love. And with all his being he learned as few of us ever do.

We in turn learn from Abraham Lincoln that greatness can grow out of ordinariness and that the capacity to love is intensified by the trauma of sorrow and suffering. We learn that patience can endure under the most aggravating circumstances and that hope and faith can survive when hopelessness seems to be all that is left.

He taught us many things, this man whom we choose to call the noblest American. But perhaps the preeminent lesson was simply this: that common clay can be molded into immortal sculpture; that our human potential is capable of almost limitless flowering and growth; and that the human soul is a widening wonder and knows no boundaries, being big enough to encompass the human race and enabling one man to be, in symbol and in fact, the Great Emancipator of us all.

"Love Thine Enemies" Why?

Love, as we have observed a number of times in these random readings, is almost as much a marvel and a miracle as the popular songs say it is. Nothing helps us give more to, or get more out of, life than that ol' black magic.

But love has an opposite number, a dark, loathsome creature called hate. And hate can tear down almost as much as love can build up. Of course we should sing, as our race always has, the glories of the one. But perhaps we should pay a little more attention than we do to the perils and pitfalls of the other.

The ugly truth is that hate is the most destructive of all emotions. It is a sinister, subversive force that pulls us away from our own true selves, and from other people, and poisons our feelings toward them or incites us to take hostile action against them. It is also the most divisive of emotions for it breaks up not only individual personalities, but homes, human relations, nations, and, twice in our century, the world. We are only beginning to understand the nightmarish things it does to personality as it tears apart the human psyche and destroys the well-springs of empathy and love.

It is quite impossible for the person who hates to be happy. To hate is to destroy one's hope of happiness and even, in any ultimate sense, to destroy oneself. If I hate you, my animosity will probably not hurt you much, but it may destroy me. By a bitter irony it may turn me from a Jekyll into a Hyde so that I become like the thing or the person I hate. The truth we have to learn about this dreadful disease is that whether it expresses itself directly or through the many disguises hate can assume, it is still a poison, destructive of body, mind and soul.

But, you may say, suppose this person you are dealing with is a mean, low-down, no-good, vindictive so-and-so. Think of all the scoundrels, bigots and tyrants who pollute the world. Am I suggesting that we ought to put aside our justifiably wrathful feelings, turn the other cheek and ignore the rotten truth so glaringly before our eyes?

Most emphatically no! Indeed, I wish more of us would work up a good healthy head of steaming hostility toward the miserable assortment of ideas, actions, attitudes and people we ought to be angry about. Sorry to say it, but the dismal fact is that there is an appalling lot in this world we ought to dislike. And one of the characteristics of the healthy mind is its ability to do precisely that: to dislike when it ought reasonably to do so.

But please note that there is a wider difference between disliking and hating then we ordinarily assume. Dislike describes our reaction to a person when we have good, sound, rational reasons for not liking him. Hate, on the other hand, implies certain obsessive sick qualities. It suggests that we have slipped over the border between reason and unreason, that blind emotion is in control and that we may even now be manifesting some of the very qualities and characteristics we so much despise in the other person.

What does all this talk about the hazards of hate add up to — that we must love our enemies? No, not necessarily, not in the usual familar meaning of the word love. But it does mean we must try not to hate our enemy (though we may hate what he does and stands for). It means that we shall respect his status as a human being with certain inalienable rights; that we must bear in mind that many of his deplorable deeds are done not so much for conscious, deliberate reasons as for unconscious, compulsive reasons (of which we may have our own fair share); and that we must strive to keep alive and to feel some sense of that warmth and relatedness that binds all human beings together and makes us members of a single human family. It may be only a spark, but as long as we can feel it and respect it, all is not lost and hate has not won.

Admittedly, this is a long way from what most of us assume the old commandment means. Yet if our poor, battered, war-torn world could rise even to the comparatively low level of this interpretation, humanity would be far better off than it has been to date and life would blossom more fruitfully because more sunlight would shine through. This may be what Balzac had in mind when he said, "Love is to the moral nature what the sun is to the earth."

How to Read the Handwriting on the Wall

How many times have you heard people say, sometimes jestingly, sometimes seriously, "Oh, if only I could read the handwriting on the wall, if only I could foretell the future!"

They say this as though they were talking about some quite impossible feat, a magic act beyond all sense or sanity. They do not seem to realize that much of the time reading the future is a surprisingly easy thing to do. The trouble is that they like the rest of us just adamantly refuse to believe what is written on the wall.

Take only a few of scores of examples from the international realm. Can any thinking person fail to read the letters-of-fire message written on the walls of the world warning us of what is almost certain to happen unless we learn to control, and really eliminate, nuclear weapons? Unless we establish world-wide dominion of the seas beneath us and the skies above us? Unless the United States and Soviet Russia overcome their manic, phobic hostility toward one another? Unless our European cousins do what wise men have urged for two thousand years and that is rise above their self-defeating national interests and establish some sort of Federation or United States of Europe? Unless our South African friends do a more pacific, reasonable job of solving their racial problem than we did here in our country little more than a century ago? Unless we Americans learn to clean up our atmosphere, reduce our deficit, increase our exports, etc.?

All right, now let's turn to the smaller personal wall each of us faces and in humility — and humiliation — see what we find. Wouldn't you think anybody with a smattering of sense would know enough to manage his or her private finances more prudently than millions of us do? After all, the handwriting is there on every bill and bank statement.

Wouldn't you think we would realize where our excessive smoking, drinking, eating, gambling, speeding are leading us? After all, the numbers are there every time we look at the scale or the speedometer. Wouldn't you think we would understand that the handwriting at the end of a continuously slovenly, sloppy job performance spells "f-i-r-e-d"?

Wouldn't you think we would have enough sense to read the medical warnings that flash through our bodies in the form of all sorts of abnormal pressures, ulcers, blurred vision, unwarranted depression and a myriad other aches and pains the flesh should not be heir to?

And here is an example which is more than simply incomprehensible, the most telling word for it is just plain stupid. Wouldn't you think all of us must realize we are going to die? Oh, come now, you say. Nobody is that witless or blind. No? Well, then consider the appalling fact that two-thirds of us Americans die without leaving a will. Because we are too thoughtless to spend an hour or two and a hundred dollars to have a will drafted (actually, you can do it yourself, though that's not advised), we cause our relatives, beneficiaries, estates a monumental assortment of headaches and problems.

China may have a Great Wall 1500 miles long. But the world's wall is far, far longer than that and the exhortations written on it are large and clear and unmistakable — or so one would think.

Here is what all of us need to understand about this business of foretelling the future: The wise man or woman is a person who reads the messages written by what Omar Khayyam called "the Moving Finger of Fate" . . . who does not shut his eyes or his mind to the tidings he sees there . . . who understands what the messages say . . . who realizes what will happen if he fails to do what they manifestly indicate he should do . . . and, finally, who has the will and the wisdom to do it.

There are few more effective ways of getting more out of life than by learning how to read — how to read the handwriting on the wall.

Sailing Lesson

The seas washed fiercely across her deck and the little yawl lay like a broken-winged bird, her hull heeled far over, pounding against the treacherous granite of Gunning Rock Shoals. Though the sail at her mizzen still flapped forlornly in the wind, she was badly smashed and beaten with a great jagged hole showing dark at her bow and I doubted that she would ever sail again. More by good luck than good judgment her crew had gotten off safely in the dinghy, but they had left behind a wreck and a warning.

Earlier that morning in the fog-bound harbor nearby, half a dozen people had warned the yawl's young skipper not to put out to sea with visibility virtually zero. But he was a foolhardy fellow and he had ignored their advice. Now that graceful shattered hull that had once been poetry running before the wind, whose white sails taut against the blue empyrean had made one's breath catch, whose perfect form and functioning had taught the mind what harmony can be, told a despairing young man more persuasively what he had already heard only a few hours before.

Nature is not cruel in the vindictive sense man sometimes is and she is not ruthless because of some interior sickness as man too often is, but she does insist that human beings recognize her laws and accept the conditions she lays down. If we do, she will permit us, even help us, to sail the seven seas with confidence and joy. If we do not, she will take our little boat and fling it uncaringly against the shoals of Gunning Rock. Nature is neither necessarily a hard taskmaster nor a cruel one, but she does demand that we accept her conditions and that we live by them.

* * * * * * * * * *

This little sea story may be taken as a kind of parable of what happens when you and I sail the even larger waters of life. Just as a sailor must know the laws of the sea and what are called "the rules of the road" (which mean the safe handling of vessels under way with respect to one another), so all of us must know something about navigation and seamanship as we sail life's bounding main.

True, the rules of life can't be codified the way traffic or fishing or boating laws can. But they exist just the same, and even more surely they exact their penalities. The fortunate ones among us who reach the Happy Isles — those tranquil, friendly harbors all of us seek — are not of a surety the strongest or wisest or wiliest. But they are the ones who have learned how to sail well and obey the laws of the sea and — no, not land — life.

What are those laws? That's not a difficult question to answer. Most of us know most of them, really. After all, their principal component is simply reasonableness or common sense. Plus an odd mix of caution and daring, free will and fatalism, intuition and a healthy lot of empirical knowledge. To be young is a time to set all sails and fly before the wind; to be old, as Emerson gently reminded us, is a time to take in sail.

But always to do either according to the sea's own

110

laws. "If wind and sky were always fair the sailor would not watch the star," said an obscure eighteenth century poet. Since the sky is never consistently fair, however, any good seaman always keeps a weather eye open and pointed skyward. The trouble is that, like that foolish young skipper, so many of us do not see the star and hear the warning the wind is calling to us or that life, kindly at first, is pressing upon us.

Let us say it again: nature . . . creation . . . life . . . are not necessarily hard taskmasters, but they do demand that we accept their conditions and that we sail, or live, by them. Some of us end up on the shoals of Gunning Rock, some on the sunny shores of the Happy Isles. So much depends on the way we trim our sails, use our heads and always listen to the "wisdom" of the wind.

On the Problem of Being Two-Faced

Sorry to break the bad news like this, but the deflating fact seems to be that all of us are two-faced. The good news is that the bad news is not as bad as it sounds.

What or whom this cryptic introduction is about is Carl Jung, one of the three seminal figures in the history of psychiatry. It was he who maintained that everybody wears two faces or has two selves. The first self he called the **persona**. This is the face or front we like to present to the world. This is our public face, so to speak. But there is also the private face or self which Jung called the **anima**. This is the self which, for better or worse, we really are.

Usually it is that first self we like to show to those around us. Naturally we want people to think we are wise, witty, attractive, generous, concerned, etc., etc. Some of us go to remarkable lengths to persuade others that this is the way we really are. And sometimes we get away with it. You must have known at least a few persons who did such a crafty selling job they succeeded in convincing the world that they were admirable, exemplary people when actually they were nothing of the sort.

Once in awhile we do manage to get away with this kind of deceit, but not very often. Somehow or other, sooner or later, we trip ourselves up and betray ourselves and, willy, nilly, that real self shows through.

As a matter of fact, there are scores of ways in which we betray ourselves and show our true colors — without ever realizing that we are doing so.

There is, for example, the way we talk about other people. It has been said the difference between gossip and news depends upon whether we heard it or told it. This is akin to a Turkish proverb, "Who gossips with you will gossip about you." Unfortunately for the tranquillity of the world, gossip appears to be more than just catty, spiteful chatter. As all of us know, there is a type of person who enjoys talking about other people, habitually in sly, suggestive, salacious terms. In doing what he does, such a person reveals an ugly area of his being. His lascivious interest in the alleged carryings-on of others suggest that secretly he would like to do the same thing himself.

Then there is the matter of humor and of what we laugh at. A sense of humor is one of humanity's most desirable qualities — assuming it's a healthy one. But there are some men and women for whom comedy and cruelty have too much in common. In the embarrassment and humiliation of others, they find something funny. They are descendants of those loutish creatures centuries ago who enjoyed watching men wrestle with, and often torn apart, by wild animals.

But of all the ways in which people disclose their true selves, surely prejudice and intolerance are the most revealing. The very fact of his bias indicates that this man may be a basically insecure person, that that woman is likely plagued by a sense of inferiority. It also suggests that both of them may have a good deal of hidden hostility and resentment toward life. Few characteristics tell us more about people than their prejudices.

Country. Religion. Moral values. Virtually all of us profess our patriotism, regard ourselves as good Christians, Jews, or whatever, and swear by the Golden Rule, the Ten Commandments and whatever other codified principles we can think of. If we truly meant what we say and lived accordingly, the world would be Utopia.

Oh, I don't mean to imply that we are all frauds and hypocrites. It is simply that too much of the time we say one thing and unawaredly do another. Or, to use Jung's language, the **persona** is supplanted by the **anima**; that cussed, embarrassing real self persists in showing through.

Remember — we reveal our true colors in many more ways than ever we know. Since this is so, may we not say the prudential as well as the right thing to do is to live our lives in such a way that when the fates trick us into showing our real selves, they will be selves of which we can be quietly proud.

More Out of Life?
One Man's Answer

All right, I may as well come clean and admit it: I am going to talk about reading. The very great importance of reading. A love of reading as one of the three or four paramount interests and delights of the thinking man or woman's life.

My problem is how to speak of a subject about which I feel so keenly in a country where a majority of the people care so little about the subject. I happen to believe that few things are a surer guarantee of enjoyment and enrichment of life than an avid, zestful love of reading. I maintain there immortal words of Sir John Herschel should be carved on Mt. Rushmore: "If I were to pray for a taste which should stand me under every variety of circumstance, and be a source of happiness and cheerfulness through life, and a shield against its ills, however things might go amiss and the world frown upon me, it would be a taste for reading . . . Give a man this taste, and the means of gratifying it, and you can hardly fail of making a happy man."

The trouble is that not enough Americans agree with Herschel and me. Do you know that fewer books (I am talking about **book** reading) are read in the United States than in almost any other developed country? That approximately half the American people never read a book (except school texts) and that less than 20 percent of our people read more than ten books a year? If Addison was right when he said "Reading is to the mind what exercise is to the body," a lot of us are in rotten shape.

It all seems so sad to me. Constantly in my professional work through the years I have encountered people who are bored, lonely, restless for something to fill their time and attention. They are Eliot's "hollow men." They are not getting much mileage out of life, and many of them know it. Well, even a finely developed love of reading might not fill such an emptiness, but one can promise it would close a lot of the hollows.

Please understand that I am not necessarily talking about Great Books courses, or the classics, or so-called serious literature. In fact, I don't much care what you read, as long as you form the habit. Once you do, you will have discovered a blissful means of relaxation and escape. Yet at the same time a more stimulating means than television provides for TV seldom engages the mind and imagination as books do.

Secondly, reading opens the doors wide to the world and all its wonders. It covers everything: people, history, travel, adventure, science, political and international affairs, romantic affairs — you name it, books will provide it.

Albert Jay Nock took another man's definition and added six words when he said, "Culture is knowing the best that has been thought and said in the world; in other words, culture means reading." Or, books mean education. Knowledge. Understanding. Wisdom. This is why a good public library may be the most precious possession we have on earth.

Aesthetic pleasures? Generally, the more one reads, the more his taste and discrimination mature.

To admire an author's ingenious development of plot or character; to relish an exquisitely polished style; to delight in a dexterously turned phrase or a perfectly chosen word: these are high on the list of the lover of reading's joys. If art is the most splendid creation of mankind, how can we enjoy that blessing more easily or fruitfully than through the satisfactions of great literature.

As for human values and illuminations, where can we learn as much, other than from experience itself. Dostoyevsky or Faulkner, Aeschylus or O'Neill, Herodotus or Morison: with impact and authority, they teach high personal, social and moral lessons. Indeed, morality has no more convincing teacher.

So, friends, my advice is this: learn to read. Learn to love reading. Learn to prize books beyond all the gold that glitters. Then you will understand the quirky wisdom of this question-and-answer:

Where can I go to get more out of life?

Go to your nearest bookstore or library!

A Rule For All the World to Follow

Throughout human history people have dreamed of a simple rule of life that would answer most of their questions and solve most of their problems. A kind of magic formula, really, that would apply in all times and places and be their **sine qua non** or one indispensable solution.

It has been a beguiling dream, alluring and seductive, and perhaps never more so than today in a time of such chaos and confusion. But it is, after all, only a dream and as resolutely as we can we must put it from us. Beware the facile, all-purpose, one-answer solution. Life is seldom that easy or that simple.

And yet . . . and yet once in a lengthy while the human race does come up with a revelation so unalloyed and true that it commands universal respect. Such a condensation of wisdom is the Golden Rule. In fact, it seems safe to say that if there is one moral principle or truth the whole world subscribes to it is this golden one. That the rule is found in all the world's great religions, and in virtually the same language at that, is of the utmost significance.

Probably the formulation most of us are familiar with is the Christian one, "Whatsoever ye would that men should do to you, do ye even so to them." But you would easily recognize the great injunction in whatever scripture you found it.

Now let's ask an obvious and intriguing question:

why has this commandment made such an enduring impression on the minds and hearts of the entire human race? Why have people in every age and place testified to its validity?

First of all, there is its blessed simplicity and reasonableness. What could be more simple and sensible than to say that we ought to treat other people the way we would like to be treated. When religion talks about Augustinianism or supralapsarianism or antidisestablishmentarianism or other such obscurities, it quickly loses most of us. But any intelligent child can understand the Golden Rule's divine common sense.

Secondly, a good deal of the principle's appeal probably centers around the fact that it has to do with doing, action, tangible results. Much of the time religion is concerned with matters of faith and belief. All of which is fine, but the prosaic fact remains that the average person is an activist. He likes to do things and see consequences and not simply speculate about them. With its injunction to act and not simply believe, the Golden Rule is speaking Everyman's language.

Next, we must consider the injunction's enormous social value. Some of the great commandments of our race have had mainly a personal or individual worth. But the Golden Rule is an altruistic decree. Altruism means regard for and devotion to the interest of others. As we live by this rule, we embark upon a process that carries us from ethics to religion and from duty to love. We are now practicing what we preach and moving from Me to Us.

But, never fear, me or I profits enormously too. The reward of a good deed lies partly in the sense of self-satisfaction, of pride in and regard for oneself that follows the doing of the deed. Psychology has demonstrated how necessary it is for each of us to feel important — in the right way. And there is no more desirable way of creating this requisite feeling of self-worth than by doing to or for others what we would have them do to or for us.

Finally, there is the beatific fact that he or she who obeys the Golden Rule provides a model that others are then likely to emulate. When we treat our fellow human beings in the manner this commandment requires, we are setting an example which is more persuasive than the commandment itself. After all, deeds teach more effectively than words. Or as Benjamin Franklin said, "None teaches better than the ant, and he says nothing."

But it was a latter-day sage, Edwin Markham, who summed up our whole commentary here when he said, "We have committed the Golden Rule to memory. Now let us commit it to life." For it is truly a golden way to get so much more from and to give so much more to life. No wonder the whole world has seen the light!

Getting More Out of Life — The Childlike Way

One of the saddest facts of human existence is that people grow up. For a man who has always stressed maturity and the maturation of the race, this may sound like a strange thing to say. When it was first published, Harry Overstreet's **The Mature Mind** had no more dedicated disciple on radio and lecture platforms than I.

What that opening sentence means, of course, is that while there are manifold childhood characteristics the truly grown-up individual leaves behind him, still there are others he retains as long as he lives and they enormously brighten and lighten his life. The misfortune of most of us is that we outgrow the characteristics we ought to retain and we retain the characteristics we ought to outgrow.

Let's face it: we grown-ups are likely to be more stuffy, conventional, unimaginative creatures than we care to believe. In order to really enjoy children, we ought to be part poet, part pixie and just plain moonstruck. Because that's the way children are. Children are anarchists, hedonists, bohemians, pagans. They are embarrassingly honest, alarmingly uninhibited and they laugh at pomposity — which is unforgivable of them. Children are as refreshing as a sea breeze, as exciting as a circus and as unpredictable as a hog on ice. Children are what we adults might be if we weren't so often stuffed shirts and old fogies.

I know I'm overstating the case a bit, but I'm doing

it to make a point — several points in fact. In the first place, the play, range and freedom of a child's imagination is one of the most refreshing things in all this mundane world. Francis Thompson once said that to be a child "is to turn pumpkins into coaches and mice into horses, lowness into loftiness and nothing into everything — for each child has his fairy godmother in his own soul."

If you want to discover what imagination can really be like, listen to the stories that children make up, on the spur of the moment and without apparent reflection. All of a sudden, that gnarled old tree in the backyard turns into a dragon, and the shadows on the lawn become giants, and you are off into a marvelous Never Never Land that would have astonished even Lewis Carroll's Alice.

Years ago when she was about six years old, our daughter Kate painted a circus picture which I think, even allowing for parental prejudice, is a perfectly delightful thing. The scene is a riot of color and action. There are trapeze artists, bareback riders, clowns, elephants and all the trimmings. There is even a zebra with five legs. Kate just got carried away with the entrancing business of painting zebra legs. I am the only man in the world who has a painting of a zebra with five legs, and I treasure it.

Paul Gauguin, that strange eccentric genius who in some respects was the father of modern painting, was fond of saying, "I paint like a child and a savage." And he did. He was an artist who never got beyond first grade, so to speak. Ordinarily, that wouldn't be much of a compliment, but in his case it is.

Another characteristic of childhood one devoutly wishes we adults might retain is the easy, natural, unaffected manner in which children accept life. La Bruyere put it this way: "Children think not of what is past, nor of what is to come, but enjoy the present time, which few of us do." How we ought to envy that blissful childhood ability to accept **this** day, and live it to the full, and squeeze the juice from it, and not worry about tomorrow. Because the normal healthy child doesn't. In this respect at least he's a stoic. Ask him about tomorrow and he shrugs his shoulders as though to say, Let tomorrow take care of itself.

Our adult reaction to such an attitude is likely to be: Well, after all, what's he got to worry about? His parents do virtually everything for him. No wonder he's so happy and carefree. But let's turn the question around and ask it of you. What have you really got to worry about? There are dozens of books available on this subject, and the principal point all of them make is that when we truly get down to brass tacks and analyze our situation, we find that the majority of us have a lot less to worry about than we think we do. If only we would devote our energies to enjoying the pleasures of **this** day and to asking the most of them, if we would stop worrying about things that will probably never happen anyhow, if we would obey Jesus' injunction to let tomorrow take care of itself, the result would be a great thing for everybody, except maybe the makers of aspirin.

No, a bonny way for us adults to get more out of life than most of us do is to be a little more childlike. (However, you will note, I trust, that the word is childlike, not childish . . .)

More About This Business of Being Childlike

When children are busy doing something they really enjoy doing, they paint picture after picture, tell story after story, and generally wear down their long-suffering parents to a pinpoint of endurance and restraint. Well, I must be practicing what I have just preached about emulating childhood's virtues because I have been so carried away with this delightful subject that I want to play with it a little longer.

Let's examine another quality children often manifest, a disarming and endearing one this time the harsh realities of life often knock out of us adults. Poets have suggested it when they have celebrated the winsome innocency and faith of childhood. Here is another of those melancholy facts about growing up: that we tend to replace trust with distrust and acceptance with suspicion. For the emotionally healthy child just naturally trusts everybody. So much so, in fact, that his parents have to warn him against going off with strangers. As Oscar Hammerstein says in **South Pacific**, "You have to be taught to hate."

At this point, some world-weary oldster is likely to say, It's all very well for children to behave in such an ingenuous fashion, but what do you suppose would happen if we adults comported ourselves in the same way? Nobody knows. But one doubts whether the world would be in any more of a mess than it's presently in. And we might just possibly fool the daylights out of ourselves. After all, people tend to react the way they are reacted to. Be friendly with a person and he or she will likely be friendly with you. Plant an apple seed and you will grow an apple tree. It would be remarkable if you grew anything else. Plant suspicion and distrust if you want to, but don't expect roses to grow from that sort of seed. It is a little disconcerting to realize that it is we adults who prate about faith, hope and love, but it is children who, in their own elemental or elementary way, more often practice these virtues.

Which brings us to a quality that is rather peculiar for the reason that it is a virtue in children but tends to be a fault in adults. I have in mind the complete candor and unabashed honesty of most young children. All of us have known grown-ups who are likely to be brutally frank, who speak their minds (or, more likely, their emotions) with little regard for the circumstances or sensitivities of others. They say things that may be honest enough, but that are less helpful than hurtful and that would be better left unsaid.

When children do the same thing, however, and say whatever they are thinking or feeling, we don't usually mind because we understand that they are not likely to be motivated by unhealthy psychological factors. There is no cutting edge to what they say. Instead, we are apt to be wryly amused and to think to ourselves, "Out of the mouth of babes and sucklings . . ."

About the same time our daughter Kate was enjoying her circus picture period, a book of mine was published. When I received my first copies, Kate picked up one of them and I told her I had written it. She was vastly less impressed than I. For quite a spell she leafed through the thing, searching for heaven knows what. Finally she looked up at me and said, "Do you really know enough to write a book?"

That was candor that I found amusing and refreshing on the part of a child, but I don't know that I would find the same query quite so amusing coming from you, and I will thank you to leave it alone.

Just as they speak their minds freely, so — and this may be their dearest characteristic of all — children give their love fully and freely. About adult love there are often elements of self-interest. Even in the case of the most adoring couple, each needs the other to complete himself or herself and for a variety of fulfilling reasons.

The love of children, however, is a more selfless, and artless, thing. "The best smell is bread, the best savor salt, and the best love that of a child," says an ancient proverb. Surely all of us have seen a child, moved by some swell of emotion, go up to a person and say "I love you," or perhaps take his hand and kiss him. Admittedly, this is not love in any grown-up evolved sense; we would be fatuous to equate it with mature love. But let's call it love anyhow for at least it is affectional response at its freest and most spontaneous.

Many sages have told us that the secret of happiness is to retain the heart of a child. To have the heart of a child is to love freely and naturally. To love in such a fashion is to be happy. The circle is complete.

126

The Four Dimensions of Life

Early in this century Albert Einstein developed his epochal special theory of relativity in which he postulated that time is the fourth dimension. I have nothing quite so world-shaking to offer, but I do think there may be some value in considering human life in these following four dimensional terms. How about length, breadth, depth and — no, not time — height.

Length. Of this quadruplet, you may be surprised to learn that the least important dimension appears to be length. Consider the ultimate senior citizen, Methuselah. Genesis says he lived 969 years. And that's about all it says. His life was of one dimension, length. Not much of a track record for a thousand year old man.

Now consider a New Testament life, one that was as full as Methuselah's was empty. Jesus of Nazareth was little more than 30 years old when the Romans executed him. Of the many dimensions of his life, length was the least important. Einstein talked about the relativity of time. In a different sense, Jesus magnificently illustrated the principle.

A contemporary of Jesus was the Roman writer Seneca. Appropriately, it was he who wrote, "We should strive not to live long, but to live rightly . . . A life is really long if it is a full life . . . Let us measure (our lives) by their performance, not by their duration."

Breadth. We Americans live in a broad land,

geographically. But how broad is it, culturally? Certainly we do not lack for cultural advantages: libraries everywhere, paperback books by the millions; cassettes and tape recorders; museums, galleries, concerts, community and regional theatres; adult education facilities of every sort; and radio, movies and television, if we use the latter judiciously.

The question, though, is how much do we take advantage of this cornucopia of culture? What figures we have are not impressive. Apparently many of us were about so broad at 20 and we are not much broader at 40 to 60. Some of us have even lost weight! (But that's another dimension.)

What a pity — to go through life like those who cannot see or hear or even feel. Socrates said, "The soul takes nothing with her to the other world but her education and culture." If Socrates was right, some of us make the journey traveling mighty light. We need to understand that living wisely means living widely; that vision is not sufficient, there must be breadth of vision; and that life is maximally full only when the arts adorn it and the mind and soul are illumined by their radiance.

Depth. In 1938 New England was devastated by one of the most savage hurricanes in the region's history. That storm was so terribly destructive because during the preceding week rain had fallen steadily. At best, New England's soil is not good holding ground, and when it was permeated by constant rainfall it could not hold its timber. Result: hundreds of thousands of trees came crashing down with a heart-splitting sound.

You and I live in a day when the great winds are

blowing hard. The aneroid barometer wavers close to 28 and some of us are being toppled like the pine and fir and birch of half a century ago. Our roots do not go down deeply enough. We have not sufficient faith or philosophy to sustain us. What our religious position may be is, of course, our business, but let us hope we have conviction and reason staunch enough to withstand even a force ten blow on the Beaufort scale. The most secure rootage is that which works its way past shallow dogmas and cultist fads down to deep universal principles that have been tested by time and affirmed by our common human experience. After, all the deeper the roots, the stronger and safer the tree.

Height. There is no Beaufort scale by which to measure true success in life, and that's too bad because too often we use the wrong criteria. We forget that bigshots are big only in the way a hot air balloon is big. This time we need to turn from down to up and ask: What did this person attempt to reach up to? What were his aspirations? What ideas and ideals motivated him? How high did he stand in the estimation of those who knew him best? Always there are lots of tall people walking around. It is just that their height, like so many virtues, is not apparent.

One thinks in this connection of William Wilberforce who early in the last century successfully led the fight for the abolition of the British slave trade. Wilberforce was a small, slight, delicate man, but in the England of his day no man stood taller.

Length, breadth, depth and height: build your life according to these dimensions and it should be able to withstand any storm . . . any trial . . . any testing.

Inferiority Feelings and
What to Do About Them

The great triumverate in the exciting pioneering days of psychiatry during the early decades of this century was Sigmund Freud, Carl Jung and Alfred Adler. Originally associates, they soon parted in disagreement and went their several ways, each man building his own school and/or comprehensive psychiatric theory.

Adler, after studying the morbid psychological problems that afflict us mortals, came to this overall conclusion: that each of us is troubled by feelings of inferiority, most of them having their genesis in early childhood situations. These inadequacy feelings are the source of much of our mental and emotional malaise or, in a word, of neurosis. Here is the root cause of that depressive, debilitating sense of worry, tension, anxiety, insecurity that, to some extent, bedevils us all.

Now, said Adler, there are two ways of coping with the inferiority problem. The healthy way is for an individual to become absorbed and involved in the larger social world around him. By making his own creative contribution to it and thus developing a sense of confidence and self-respect, he compensates for and, to that extent overcomes, his inferiority feelings. Therefore it is necessary that we have the right kinds of goals in life and that we resolutely move toward them.

The unhealthy way to relate to our problems is in a self-contained and private fashion. By ignoring our social obligations and opportunities, we reject the very means that could help us supplant inferiority with the right kind of superiority feelings, and our neurotic symptoms are only exacerbated. All of us have a legitimate need for power and self-assertion, but that need must be met in constructive ways.

As the twentieth century has wended its turbulent way toward wherever it is going, inevitably the original (and wonderfully innovative and insightful) theories of the founding fathers have been modified considerably. Like Freud's primacy-of-sex concept, Adler's inferiority complex has been cut down to a more reasonable size. Yet one has to concede that there is a lot of pep and vinegar in the old complex still. Who is so self-deceptive that he refuses to admit, at least privately, that inferiority feelings have not only plagued him, but have sporadically determined his behavior and his life?

Well, if such is indeed the case and Adler was on to something pretty basic here, what can we do about the problem he poses? Several things. For one, we can concentrate more of our attention on the special aptitudes and abilities all of us have, on our superiorities, if you will. And, as we have seen elsewhere in this tome, everybody does have them. In some cases, the trouble is just that we haven't discovered our potentialities; in more cases, it is simply that we haven't bothered to do much with them.

Adler talked a good deal about compensation, by which he meant that in seeking to overcome inferiorities we are likely to develop superiorities. And of course that's great. Whatever the unconscious motivations and mechanisms may be, let's drink a toast to compensation. And let's go a little further and **consciously** seek to grow in those areas where growth is most likely for us. Few experiences in life provide more satisfaction than doing a thing and doing it well.

Orthodox theologians may rail against hubris, or pride, as one of the most heinous of sins. But that is excessive of them, to put it gently, because pride, the right kind of pride, the pride that is confidence and satisfaction with one's own abilities, is, as Adler demonstrated, an indispensable quality of the healthy life.

Then we can do this blessedly therapeutic thing. For centuries the saints and prophets have urged us to get outside of ourselves and find the deeper meaning of our lives in other lives and in causes and purposes more ample than our own small selves. They have done this for essentially religious reasons.

But now here are Adler and psychiatry in general saying approximately the same thing, only this time for psychological reasons. Never mind who says it, though, the principle is valid in whatever case. When we set worthy goals and seek to achieve them and when they have a broad social and/or religious significance, we are on the high road to that healthiness of mind and spirit than which there is no greater blessing.

Adapt — Or Else!

When two people live as close to the sea, summer and winter, as my wife and I do, they are bound to learn some pretty fundamental lessons from the experience. For the sea is a compelling teacher. For instance, sometimes the sea just starkly says, Adapt — or else! And that "or else" may be followed by the burbling sound a sailor or a ship makes as either slowly slips beneath the waves. It is a prudent policy to learn one's nautical lessons.

Here is a lesson we learn and relearn each summer. It is simply called "Adapt." Few faculties of sea life and the sea are more impressive than their almost limitless capacity for adaptation. Study any form of salt water life along the Maine coast — kelp or wrack or eelgrass, the mollusks or crabs or limpets or sea urchins or lobsters or whatever — and you will find that when the environment changes, the organism somehow accommodates itself and changes too. For three or four billions of years now life has managed to survive in the sea because of its amazing ability to adapt itself to the changing conditions of its environment.

Consider three examples from the shores of our place on Maple Juice Cove. As you may know, spring tides have no connection with the season of the year that we call spring. They are just unusually high and low tides that occur twice a month at the time of the new and the full moon. This means that twice, and only twice, a month we have a little strip of shoreline that is almost always under water except for a few hours every four weeks when it is exposed to light and air. So what has happened? So a form of seaweed has developed that requires air only twice a month.

Example number two. At the lower levels of our shore when the tide is out one finds the so-called common periwinkle, a form of snail. Halfway up the shore at midtide line one finds the smooth periwinkle. And on the upper half of our shore the rough periwinkle abounds. Here is a little mollusk that has so ingeniously adapted itself to the demands of its life that on 25 feet of our shoreline between high and low tides you will find three different varieties.

Example number three. The bottom of our cove is literally paved with blue mussels, which are first cousin to a clam (and, we think, even more delicious). Down on the mucky bottom are hundreds of thousands of them. Reaching out into the waters of the cove are also many rocks and ledges, and eons ago the mussels would have been swept against the rocks and crushed if they had not developed thread-like filaments that loosely attach them to the rocks, rather like the guy ropes of a tent.

But that isn't all they have done. In order to resist the force of the sea, the mussel shell ought to have its narrow end facing the tide or the waves. So again what has happened? So the threads by which the mussel attaches itself to the rock are arranged in such a way that the mussel can turn about and present its streamlined side to the pressure of the sea. Thus it resists both the threat of the rocks and the pounding of the sea.

What we have illustrated here is one of the foundation principles of life on this planet. It is the ineluctable fact that that which cannot, or will not, accommodate itself to change and challenge is doomed to die. And as we ought to understand more clearly than many of us do, this is a principle that applies quite as inexorably to people, nations, civilizations, the universe itself as it does to eelgrass, periwinkles and mussels. And when the pace of life quickens to today's dizzying speed, we must become more than ever adept as quick-change artists.

In such a whirligig world as ours, one of the few all-encompassing conclusions one feels safe in coming to is that the future of human society depends upon nothing so much as our ability to do what life has been doing for perhaps four billion years and that is — adapt. **But fast!** We do not have the option of dealing in ages, eons and epochs. We have to take the latest wonderwork in the evolutionary process, the human mind, and surely and swiftly use it to effect the kinds of melioration, change, progression that are really our only instruments of salvation. The key factors here are understanding and rapidity of action. Today it is not enough to change, that change must occur as quickly as possible because, to put it as simply as possible, of the alternative . . .

So — don't forget our crustaceous lessons from the seashore. All the savants and sages put together could not teach us more basic or more imperative ones. Three examples in three words: Adapt — or else!

The Problem With Telling
the Truth

When we talk in serious speculative terms about meaning in life, we often find ourselves using such words as freedom, love, loyalty, purpose, goodness, truth. Truth. About this last value or virtue I have always liked something Daniel Webster said, "There is nothing as powerful as truth — and often nothing as strange."

What I have in mind here is that many of us take truth too much for granted. We assume that truth exists, which of course it does. But then we also assume it is something as simple and easy to know as that night follows day, that harvest follows planting. We do not follow Webster who said that there is "often nothing as strange." Let me tell you about a lesson I have learned from the sea that has taught me to be wary of talking about truth too casually or thoughtlessly.

People who are not familiar with the sea sometimes assume that sailing it must be a simple proposition: one simply follows his compass until it leads him to wherever he wants to go. What such people forget, or never know, is that a compass does not point to true north, it points to the magnetic north. This is called variation and it means that through the use of a special plotting device known as a "compass rose" the compass must be corrected.

Then there is a second complication called deviation. On almost any boat, certain fixed metal objects tend to deflect the compass needle. By a process known as "swinging ship," the skipper must determine what the degree of deviation is for his particular vessel and again make the indicated correction.

But compass error is not the only problem involved in navigating a boat. Wind can, and frequently does, push a boat in any direction it pleases. Unbeknownst to the casual skipper, tidal forces can move his craft all over the sea. Then there are vast ocean currents that often have their way willy-nilly with any vessel they encounter.

The point is that sailing the sea is not as simple a process as it may sometimes seem.

The corollary, and greater, point is this: that truth too involves more navigational problems than we usually realize. A person says, I have found the truth. But has he made sure that his compass is pointing to true and not magnetic north? Has he corrected for the invisible influence of deviation? Has he taken into account the mighty marine forces of wind and wave and ocean current?

Of course there is such a thing as truth, and no doubt a person can find it. But a word of caution, if you please. Just remember that searching for truth, like sailing the sea, is not as simple a matter as it may often appear.

Truth, we say, is what conforms with reality. And a first-rate definition that is. But what about those of us in a culture that frequently prefers fantasy to reality, whether in romance and religion, or domestic policies and foreign affairs, or private reveries and Presidential daydreams? "Great is the truth and shall prevail" says one of the Apocryphal books, 11 Esdras, and I believe it. But I also believe that much of the time the going for poor old truth is rougher than ever we know. Indeed, so tortuous is the route that to this day philosophies and religions can only occasionally agree on whatever it is they mean by that elusive reality, "the truth."

He was a haunted romantic who probably knew more about the sea than he did about the truth. Even so, Lord Byron was perceptive enough to take Webster's thought and recast it in his own lyric fashion: " 'Tis strange but true, for truth is always strange — stranger than fiction."

The Calculated Risks of Life

Gambling is a game, risk, addiction that generally has a bad name among us. And I have no intention of risking my good name by serving as a shill for Las Vegas. On the other hand, I believe that before we convict and pass sentence, we ought to give even a disreputable word a fair trial. And one of the things about trials, as you know if you have watched many movies, is that they are full of surprises.

The surprise in this case is that gambling, far from being a villain, is often a virtue. A very substantial virtue. Indeed, if we are going to make of our lives what we could and should make, it is a necessary virtue. There is simply no way of creating a full and fruitful life without taking those risks and chances which are otherwise known as gambles. What is falling in love and marrying but a gamble? (If you don't believe this, the divorce statistics should quickly convince you.) What is having a family but a gamble? Any one, or all, of your children may die and break your heart as nothing else could. Friendship is a gamble, business is a gamble, free elections are a gamble. In very short, life itself is a gamble.

We present-day Americans simply do not realize what an enormous, unparalleled risk the founding of our country was. Except for a small experiment in Greece more than 2000 years before, there had never been anything like it in human history. Most of the world, including many of our own predecessors right here in the colonies, thought what was happening was crazy. Even that inveterate optimist, Benjamin Franklin, confessed that during the Constitutional Convention he looked at the sun carved on the back of the presiding officer's chair and wondered whether it was a rising or a setting sun.

The dicey fact is it was a gamble without precedent and against intimidating odds. Yet so successfully did our forefathers win the gamble that they changed the course of history, and for the vastly better and brighter. Because they risked their freedom and their lives, a new age began and civilization moved appreciably forward.

In fact, one of the distinctive things about democracy is its riskiness. It is a considerably more risky venture than communism. Reluctance to change; heavy restraining walls, both physical and philosophical; fear of untried ways, ideas, dreams — these are the hallmarks of the hammer-and-sickle, not of the stars-and-stripes.

And what is true of our government is true of our economy. Basic to it is something we call risk capital, which is just what its name says it is: money invested in usually new and unproven ventures. But communism, an ideology which supposedly believes that economics is the motor that drives history, cares little for such capricious practices. Like Henry Ford who preferred to stick with his outmoded Model T and thus lost leadership of the American automobile industry to upstart General Motors and its newfangled improvements, the Kremlin predictably opts for the tried and, presumably, true. Capitalism seems to work best when it is reasonably unfettered and is allowed to take chances. Its gambles sometimes fail, of course, but when they succeed, they strengthen and improve the economy as nothing else can.

Government . . . economics . . . and now people. There are some of us who pose a peculiar kind of personality problem. Possibly as children we gave ourselves openly, as children are wont to do, only to be rejected and shut out. When we tried to express affection for our parents, they did not respond. When we attempted to make friends with other children, they laughed at us in the unintentional but cruel way children sometimes have. So in self-defense we retreated behind our own barricades and would not risk being hurt or rejected any more. Life and love were propositions we were no longer willing to gamble on.

What a tragedy! For one of the animating truths of our race is that people are most alert and alive when they are being daring, taking chances, risking their all in behalf of great-hearted causes. If they win, wonderful!, the earth turns a little more surely on its axis. And even if they lose, they know it is better to have loved and lost than never to have loved at all, better to risk much and to gain much than to risk nothing and to gain what they risked. For this is the way that progress is made and the world advances — through the calculated risks of the strong of mind and the stout of heart.

A Different Definition
of Happiness

A number of times through the years people have asked me what my definition of happiness is. I have replied that of course there is no single definition that can satisfy everybody, but here is one I like especially: Happiness is doing something that you like to do, that is worth doing, and that you do well. (A modest man, I usually neglect to mention that one reason I may admire these words so uncommonly is that I am their author.)

They have been for me not so much a definition as a gradual discovery or revelation through the years. Increasingly I have come to realize that when I am doing something I like to do and do well, I feel a sense of satisfaction, fulfillment and self-confidence that adds up to what I choose to call happiness.

That many, perhaps most, people do not so choose, I am quite aware. To them, happiness is much more closely identified with merrymaking, laughter, fun, play, games, vacations and the like. Or, in a little more sober and personal fashion, with peace of mind, tranquility, family, friends, being with someone they love. In no way do I disparage their conceptions; I like and go along with them all.

But over the long haul, as a day-by-day satisfaction, as a source of continuing pleasure, I think it is difficult to beat my number one choice, creativity. This is so far removed from what most people think of as happiness that it takes a bit of interpreting, so let me give you a not very pleasant illustration.

Perhaps the most harrowing punishment that can be imposed on a person in prison is to put him in solitary confinement. Most people miss the real point, or pain, of the discipline. They assume it lies in the solitude, in the void created by the absence of other human beings. But, surprisingly, the real punishment is simply the desolation of having nothing to do.

In a negative way, the anguish of the solitary prisoner in his empty cell gives us an affecting notion of the psychological importance and purpose of creativity. Doing almost anything is better than doing nothing. The opposite of work is not so much play as an apathy and emptiness that can lead a person, figuratively and literally, to self-destruction.

One of the most enervating weaknesses of American society these days is the constantly dwindling number of jobs that involve creative work. More and more of our commodities are machine and/or mass-produced. Far more of us today than ever before are working in white-collar or service jobs where we shuffle papers or fiddle with instruments or take in each other's wash. The satisfaction of the artisan who could see and feel and admire his day's work in his hands or before his eyes is a kind of well-being and fulfillment few of us any longer enjoy.

It was Sigmund Freud, not much of an artist or artisan himself, who, with his theory of the libido, helped us understand the inestimable importance of what we have been saying here. He maintained that every human being has within him all sorts of generative urges and impulses which Freud subsumed under this term "libido." Sex may be the primary force, but he included all of an individual's creative impulses, and he claimed that when these demands are not satisfied, that man or woman is likely to become psychologically, or neurotically, ill. On the other hand, when they are fullfilled, he or she experiences the sense of achievement and consummation I have identified with happiness.

Like many of Freud's theories, this one was somewhat overblown, yet it has an essential truth you can assess for yourself. Think back over your life to those times when you were engaged in a task you did well and enjoyed doing. It doesn't much matter whether it was painting a picture, cooking or sewing, building a business, supervising a department, teaching a responsive class, or even, believe it or not, painting the guest bedroom. While you were doing it and directly after, you felt a gratification and satisfaction that can cheerily be called the joy of creativity.

There are many joys we human beings are privileged to experience, and we do not usually place this one up at, or near, the top of the list. But think about it for a spell, and then move it up the scale. To do whatever one is doing well, to do it to a worthwhile end, and to enjoy doing it. I am not contending that this is the most blissful or the ultimate happiness. I am simply saying that in down-to-earth, everyday terms it may be the most satisfying and sustaining.

"The Red Badge of Courage"

On almost any list of the dozen most significant American novels you are likely to find **The Red Badge of Courage**. And no wonder. It is an astonishing book, unique in our literary history. For instance, its author, Stephen Crane, was just 24 years old when the book was published in 1895. How anyone so young could write so knowingly and brilliantly is a major mystery.

The Red Badge of Courage is the story of a boy who joins the Union Army during the Civil War. Here again, an enigma. Stephen Crane had never been in combat, had never had any exposure to the horrors of war. Yet few writers of whatever day have conjured into life as he did the nightmarish sights, sounds, terrors and torments of battle.

Then there is the revealing fact that Crane was one of the first American realists or naturalists. Rebeling against the sentimental tradition and recognizing that war is hell, he determined to say so. Not to shock people, but because that's the way war is, an inferno of blood, spilled guts and agonizing death; tragically, but truly, that's reality. Dying as he did in 1900, Crane helped open the way for a new twentieth century kind of American writing.

The protagonist of his story is simply called The Youth, although in a sense he might be called Everyman for a reason we shall soon see. Relentlessly, The Youth is haunted by a single question: When he goes into battle, will he have the courage to endure, or will he lose his nerve, break and run?

Only too soon, his question is answered. In their first engagement, he and his regiment stand firm — at first — and The Youth rejoices. But then, unfairly, the Rebels attack again, and this time The Youth and some of his companions break and flee in mindless panic.

Now begins one of the most memorable passages in American literature. All that afternoon and evening he wanders broken-heartedly, believing himself a coward and that every man can see the yellow stain upon him. What reader who has accompanied the boy on his passage can ever forget his ghastly encounter with a corpse, leaning against a tree, the body dreadfully decomposed, that seems to rise up and follow him like the ghost of his own conscience.

Finally he finds his way back to his regiment, mercifully he learns that he has not been missed and he lies down on the ground and sleeps the sleep of the dead. When he wakes in the morning, he discovers that somehow, mysteriously, he has changed. "A faith in himself had secretly blossomed . . . He was now a man of experience. He had been out among the dragons and he assured himself that they were not so hideous as he had imagined them."

When the regiment goes into battle again a few hours later, this time The Youth fights like a man possessed. When his companions are fearful of making another charge, he leaps out in front of them, seizes the regiment's flag, and with a bandage covering a slight head wound, with his red badge of courage, he leads the troops to victory.

After the storm has passed, he sits on the ground and meditates. "He saw that he was good . . . He knew that he would no more quail before his guides wherever they should point . . . He was a man . . . So it came to pass as he trudged from the place of blood and wrath his soul changed. Scars faded as flowers."

Any true work of art tells us a surprising lot about ourselves; it illumines our common human experience. **The Red Badge of Courage** says that no human being is always a hero. All of us are sometimes guilty of indiscretions, weaknessess, shameful conduct. To put it as bluntly as a beating, there are times when all of us are cowards. This is a part, an embarrassingly yet bitterly real part, of what it means to be a human being.

But now remember who The Youth is. He is not some classic hero out of Greek mythology. He's just an ordinary guy, he could be either Yankee or Rebel; he is Everyman. And what does he do? After he breaks and runs, he recovers himself, returns and, from those secret reserves of courage all of us have, he finds the strength to stand forth and lead the charge.

The message of this book is not that ordinary people are cowards, which we sometimes are, but that we can be heroes, which we also are more often than we know. We do not need a red badge of courage, you and I, for the evidence of our fortitude is clearly to be seen in everything we say and do and are. Courage is not only "grace under pressure," it is also the strength to dare the challenges of life, and by so doing, as The Youth did, come to know a confidence unshakable and a peace that passes understanding.

Getting More Out of Life:
Is Utopia the Answer?

Ever since recorded history began, a persisting dream has haunted the human mind, a wistful dream usually, a beautiful dream always. It is a vision of an ideal society whose people exist under the most nearly perfect conditions possible. It is what Josiah Royce called "the Beloved Community," a fellowship where all live together in peace, justice, equity, security and contentment. Sometimes even pain and disease have been eliminated so that what results is a fair approximation of a kingdom of heaven on earth.

The first fully developed version of the dream was Plato's **Republic** 2500 years ago. Through the ensuing centuries, some of our loftiest literature has been utopian: Augustine's **City of God**, Sir Thomas More's **Utopia** (a name More coined from two Greek words which means "no place"), Francis Bacon's **New Atlantis** (an early version of a scientific paradise), Samuel Butler's **Erewhon** (which is "nowhere" misspelled and written backward) and, in our time, stories like H.G. Wells' and novels like Hilton's **Lost Horizon**.

But we visionary humans have not only written about Utopia, we have attempted to establish it. The nineteenth century here in America was notable for the number of idealistic communal experiments we undertook. One of them was the Amana Colony in Iowa which my father studied extensively and which, as a boy, living in nearby Cedar Rapids, I came to know well.

The reasons why men and women have persisted in their attempts to create a more nearly ideal society must be so obvious we needn't bother to discuss them. What we should ask, however, is this: have they been generally successful and, if not, why not?

A summary answer is no. With few exceptions, our utopian social experiments, always begun with the highest of hopes, have ended, most of them sooner than later, in disarray and disillusionment. Here again at least part of the reason is easily understood. Imperfect people, which we are, have a lot of trouble conforming to perfectionist demands. Like children, we find it difficult to be **that** good. There is typically an artificial, unnatural quality about the Utopian situation that makes us uncomfortable and finally unsatisfied. Despite all its faults and failings, we prefer this battered old world the way it defectively is.

An even more serious problem is this: whether they are aware of the fact or not, utopian experiments tend to be totalitarian. From Plato's **Republic** to Hilton's Shangri-la, you will find an authoritarian pattern. There really has to be one. If you want people to conform to certain dictates, if you want to achieve perfection in a hurry, you can probably do so most quickly at the point of a gun. Or at least by setting up a system of rules and regulations, of disciplines and demands, that has a disconcerting lot in common with dictatorship. Sloppy, inefficient, exasperatingly slow, the democratic process simply will not do.

Through the centuries, the utopian dream has been a noble one (even if its implementation has been somewhat less than exemplary). Perhaps we may say that its principal value has been an inspirational rather than a practical one. Every sensible, responsible human being ought to have some notion of what a more nearly ideal society, a Utopia, if you will, might be like, and he or she has a solemn social obligation to help realize that vision. It is simply that the ameliorative, gradual, democratic way seems to most of us a more reasonable one than the swift, intolerant, totalitarian way.

The old fables and fantasies of a Lost Atlantis, a City of the Sun, Oceana, Icaria, Camelot make fascinating reading. They hover in the minds as legends of lost Edens do. But at the end, a little plaintively, perhaps, we have to close the book and return to this untidy real world of real, ordinary, fallible human beings. Thornton Wilder titled one of his books **Heaven Can Wait**. But maybe . . . just maybe if each of us does as much as he can in his own, not necessarily small, way to bring utopian dream and everyday reality a little closer together, maybe heaven won't have to wait quite so long as one might think.

Reassurance

A number of times in these little essays I am assaying here, I have spoken of the harrowing sense of uncertainty and misgiving that afflicts so many of us moderns. Religion and philosophy have always been concerned with the great ontological, teleological and cosmological questions of being, purpose, meaning, existence. In the past, we were never sure of the answers (except as orthodoxies provided them); in the present, we are even less sure. We do not know where we came from, why we are here, or where we are going. We wander apprehensively through a world in which the old absolutes have disappeared and everything seems relative and conditional. The result is a free-floating anxiety that strikes to the very root of our being. It is a sense of alienation, of being cut off from that which gives substance and significance to life and the universe. It comes close to what some theologians have defined as hell.

Just as surely as the next person, I am disturbed and anxiety-haunted too. Much of the time. But I want to tell you about those occasions when my tension eases and I find something of that alleviating, undergirding security for which all of us hunger. That sense that there are foundations that will not, cannot be shaken.

For instance, I think few phenomena are likely to give a person a more sustaining awareness of continuity and reassurance than the way ocean tides ebb and flow, ebb and flow, predictable all over the world right down to the last minute. In our kitchen at Maple Juice Cove we have a tide table. It's a cross between a calendar and a timetable. I can look at that thing on May 16th and tell you that on the following December 16th at nearby Rockland high tide will be at 7:31 a.m, low tide at 1:43 p.m. You'd be surprised what a reassurance that little compendium of figures is.

Then, when the tide permits, I love to walk the shoreline of our place, situated as it is with the sea on three sides. The granite rock beneath my feet was formed, as best as we know, back when the earth was cooling in the dawn days of creation. Attached to the rock the seaweed that we call bladder and knotted wrack sways in the tide and dries in the sun just as it did eons before the brontosaur and the tyrannosaur roamed the earth. A dragonfly skimming about my head has fossilized ancestors 35 million years old, and a tern wheeling above my head dives straight down into the water just as his ancestors dove, how many million years ago.

In the sea itself, only inches beyond my feet, are a myriad of creatures whose kind has survived virtually unchanged since the days when the world was young and life was only a sort of tentative experiment: sponges and jellyfish, worms of many kinds, snail-like mollusks and barnacles, sea urchins, crabs and lobsters.

And then when I go outside at night and look above me, there just as they have been for an infinity of time, are Castor and Cygnus and Pollux, and Cassiopeia's

Chair, and the Great Square of Pegasus with Andromeda floating along in the left-hand corner.

Perhaps what I am saying here with all this seashore reminiscence is that nature helps us feel in a visceral way what religion tells us in a metaphysical and science in a physical way. As thinking creatures we have to be concerned about the great cosmological questions intellectually, with our minds; but there is a sense in which we must also perceive them existentially and experientially with our bodies and spirits.

These are big words, but all they mean is that a person must not only know, he must also feel, and when it is a question of alleviating our transcendental anxieties, feeling is the more essential.

In any event, when the prevailing southwest wind blows across the ocean and our cove — I say this again — it seems to carry away with it a fair measure of my apprehensions and insecurities, and I stand out under the midnight sky feeling sure and secure as I do at no other time, in no other place.

This Strange New World
in Which We Live

It has become a commonplace — you must have heard or read it a score of times — for writers and public speakers to remark that the world has changed more in the two hundred years between George Washington's day and our own than it changed in the eighteen hundred years between Washington's time and that of Jesus of Nazareth. In fact, it has changed so far and so fast that even the wisest of us cannot comprehend the full significance of what has happened.

Try to imagine Washington's reaction if he could have been removed from his coach-and-four and whisked away on a flight in a 747 airplane. Then multiply that example by thousands, some of them, like the nuclear one, even more incredible, and you may have a shadowy notion of the fantastic transformations that have been taking place.

Well, we needn't belabor the point. Even the more obtuse among us must have some awareness of the kaleidoscopic, speed-of-light times in which we live. The question we have to ask ourselves is how can we not only survive in such a tumultuous time, but find enhanced meaning — and value and reason for being — in it?

First of all, we can join what Norman Cousins called the Unthinkables. He had in mind the nuclear threat. He did not mean that we mustn't think about it; he meant that we must regard it as a totally unacceptable, or unthinkable, option. And clearly we must. Even the most militant hawks concede that a major nuclear war would be the end of the race — the human race, that is.

It is true that we have let the genie out of the bottle, that it is easier to develop a nuclear bomb than it is to control it, that people bedeviled by fear and suspicion are not the most reliable judges of what to do. Nevertheless, we **have** to do what **must** be done. If **vox populi** has any meaning, if the voice of the people carries the authority it should have, and must have, in a democracy, then let us speak out and speak the Unspeakable.

But do we have the necessary insight, knowledge, wisdom? By heaven, we had better have! And the saving evidence is that we do. Anthropologists sometimes maintain that a, or the, principal difference between us and the other animals is that we are problem-solving creatures. By being able to think rationally, objectively and, latterly, scientifically, we have made possible the glories of civilization. Who created language, religious precepts, ethics, philosophy, social principles, government, the arts, the healing sciences? We did! And we have done it all in the span of only a few thousand years.

If you want to get some sense of what we have truly accomplished, don't go to the Space Center at Houston, impressive as that surely is. Go to our libraries, museums, more enlightened churches, social service centers, medical laboratories, international institutes and great universities. Then your faith in the human potential will be exultantly strengthened and you will feel less fear and a good deal more faith in the human potential.

Now there is one more thing we must all do. Studies indicate that Americans today are about 2½ inches taller than our countrymen were a hundred years ago, and the expectation is that the average person will soon be six feet tall. Physically, that is. There is one dimension, however, in which we are going to have to grow even faster and taller. For want of any other term, I think we must call it the spiritual sphere. It is awe-inspiring, but not sufficient, that we have developed minds capable of sending rockets to the ends of the universe. Now we must develop hearts, souls, spirits capable of hearing John Donne's bell tolling and of traveling to the ends of the earth because love and compassion know no bounds.

It has become another commonplace to say that our material and scientific progress has outdistanced our moral and spiritual progress. If that is true, as it seems to be, then it is evident that humanity's most imperative task from now on must be to develop our spiritual potential, our capacity for service, sacrifice, empathy, devotion, love. That we have the capacity to do so there can be no doubt. What we must now do is open the floodgates of our hearts as we have un-leashed the potentialities of our minds. For the human spirit, sensitive, compassionate, concerned, rising to meet the challenges of this strange new modern world as life rises from darkness to greet the dawn, it is that spirit that is at once our promise and our only hope.

Getting More Out of Two Lives

Probably the most common remark our friends make about my wife and me is that we live in the best of two worlds. And in both instances along glamorous coasts. Summers find us in the picturesque Camden-Rockland-Thomaston area of mid-coast Maine. Winters we bask on that picture postcard strand of Florida sand, sea and sun called the Gold Coast which stretches from Miami to the Palm Beaches.

Friends envy us. And well they might. It would be difficult to find two more idyllic regions in which to spend our lives, winter and summer.

But the question that arises here in connection with the subject of our book is this: given the two-fold advantage or life-style Isabel and I enjoy, are we getting twice as much out of life as we otherwise would? In a sense, it might seem as though we should. If one pleasant retreat is good, two pleasant retreats ought to be twice as good.

The arithmetic here seems reasonable enough, but of course the trouble with arithmetic is that it has nothing to do with human meanings and motives. Two and two may add up to four, but a villa in Cannes, an apartment in Paris, a summer home in Bar Harbor and a ski lodge in Aspen do not necessarily add up to four times as much happiness. We have all read of celebrities and ultra wealthy types who own more glamorous property around the world than the Hilton-Sheraton-

Marriott interests combined. Yet from what evidence shows through the tinsel and sequins, they seem little happier than the rest of us mere mortals.

Actually, of course, there is no particular mystery involved here. Reflective, intelligent people have known for ages that there is no hard-and-fast correlation between wealth and felicity, between riches of the flesh and riches of the spirit. In fact, if you care to listen to the wisest of men and women on the subject, like Socrates, the Buddha, the writer of Ecclesiastes, Jesus, Epictetus, much of the Talmud, Marcus Aurelius, St. Francis, George Fox, Mother Teresa and most of the other saints, you may come to the demoralizing conclusion that far too many of us, like those dreadful creatures, the Spanish conquistadors, have been searching down the wrong roads for the wrong prizes.

The literature of religion is a cautionary collective reminder that wealth, like quicksilver, is slippery stuff to handle; that where your bankbook is, there your heart may also be; that (this is a splendid piece of imagery) a camel can get through a needle's eye more easily than a rich man can get into the kingdom of heaven. Or, as a modern version has it, that it is about as hard for a rich man to enter heaven as it is for a poor man to remain on earth.

But before we don sackcloth and ashes, sell off our Xerox and IBM and turn over the deed of our beloved Camp Wa-De-Da to the Salvation Army, let's pull up short and observe one enormously important fact. The problem here is not the magnitude of our wealth, the problem is our attitude toward it. Many of the most generous, altruistic, compassionate men and women

I have known have been wealthy people. They remind me of that typically Shavian comment of GBS when he said it is not true that wealth makes people intemperate and self-centered. On the contrary, it is poverty that makes them miserly and mean-spirited. Or I think of James Russell Lowell's remark made in a Harvard anniversary address, "Wealth may be an excellent thing, for it means power, it means leisure, it means liberty."

May not the resolution of this whole business be suggested by these words: A primary test of character is how one handles one's worldly goods. The familiar French phrase **noblesse oblize** means "nobility obligates." What we must understand is that wealth does too. It may be ours, but it is ours to share, to use generously, thoughtfully, humanely. Wealth obligates. Fail to understand that and you have failed one of life's most basal tests.

So — appreciate, enjoy and share what you have; be grateful that the fates have smiled benignly upon you, and you should be able to live steadfastly and serenely in however many worlds you are privileged to inhabit.

"The Constant Joy of Sudden Discovery"

Four hundred and ninety-five years ago Columbus discovered America. He did better than a lot of us do. There are too many people who have lived in this country all their lives, and yet they have never discovered America — or very much else, for that matter. To become a discoverer, not of new continents, but of new ideas, insights, interests and skills is still another way, and a specially satisfying and enjoyable way, of getting more out of life.

A case in point is this little story about a well-known Texas writer and teacher who as a young man traveled to New York City to study. One day, wandering through the Metropolitan Museum of Art, he noticed a picture that impressed him especially. It was a snow scene, and some of the snow was rose-colored, really a kind of purple. Coming as he did from the lower part of Texas, he had never seen much snow. And, naturally enough, he had always assumed that snow is — snow-white.

Some weeks later he took a walk in the woods over in the Jersey countryside. All of a sudden, he saw something he had wondered about ever since that museum visit. Under some bushes, partly in shadow, he saw — rose-colored snow!

The young Texan made an important discovery that winter afternoon. He learned that if a man keeps his eyes open and his mind alert he can discover all sorts of odd, delightful, fanciful things everywhere about him. I am not a painter, but I have had a life-long association with painters and painting, and I think I have learned something choice from those experiences. As I have remarked elsewhere in this book, I have learned that there is not one, there are really many intriguing and imaginative ways of seeing the most familiar object. It is an ability all good artists have and that children don't need to acquire; lucky them, they seem to have it as naturally as flowers bloom.

Let us assume that here on this table are a few pieces of fruit in a bowl. One artist will be particularly impressed with the color he sees, and on his canvas great sunbursts of orange and lemon and green will blaze forth. Another artist, pleased by the forms of the fruit, will produce a painting in which color is de-emphasized and where configuration, shape, structure are the essential qualities. Still another artist, noticing a shadow falling across a corner of the table, will decide to accentuate the play of light and dark, of black and white — he will adumbrate the scene, so to speak. And so on and on and on. For the fact is that there is an almost endless variety of ways to represent these commonplace objects.

Musical and literary history are replete with examples of much the same sort of perceptiveness. Through the centuries, composers have perked up their heads to catch the simple melody of a children's song, and writers have suddenly heard or seen something provocative within and beyond the familiar children's story, or folktale, or legend, or saga. In that elementary material, they have discovered ampler melodies and meanings. The result has been some of our most inspired music and literature, great rivers rising from tiny springs, rare blooms blossoming from common seed. It is what Mencken called "the constant joy of sudden discovery."

Most of us are familiar with Henry Thoreau's sly observation that he had "traveled a good deal in Concord," a characteristically Thoreauvian way of saying that he had discoverd a lot in a little place. Not far away, in another charming New England village, Emily Dickinson made the same expansive discovery. At the close of this book there is a parable about a man who found everything he wanted or needed in his little haven by the sea. What all of them teach us — artists, poets, philosophers, children finding endless fascinations in their own backyard — is that the raw materials of surprise and delight are everywhere about us. Maybe because it is so simple and so true, and because it is like a little light burning in my mind, I have always remembered a line from Emerson's essay "Nature": "Most people do not see the sun." Or there is William James: "Genius, in truth, means little more than the faculty of perceiving in an unhabitual way."

Rose-colored snow . . . the melodies of bird song . . . castles of cloud more marvelous than Xanadu . . . places even more wonder-full than Thoreau's Concord or Dickinson's Amherst: all we need are eyes that see, ears that hear and minds that appreciate, and **voila!**, ours is "the constant joy of sudden discovery."

Lessons of a Traveling Man

During my lifetime, I have traveled in many parts of the globe. When I have talked about my travels, people have understandably asked me what I have learned from them. And I have spoken of a few of the mind-expanding experiences I have had and of some of the far-off colorful (and decidedly not so colorful!) places I have visited.

But, after all, the important thing about this world of ours is not so much places as people. So I have usually opted to talk about the latter. And I have begun by confessing my initial surprise. No matter how well educated he may be, before a person has traveled much abroad, I suspect there is likely to be a notion at the back of his mind that people in other countries are a little different, and sometimes a good deal different, from us. And of course when he gets over to the other side of the world, he will find a sunburst of differences.

But my experience has taught me that that notion is about 90 percent false. In fact, at first one is somewhat disappointed. He gets off a ship at Yokohama or an airplane at Rangoon expecting, well, certainly something a little diverse, presumably foreign and, preferably, exotic. But a few hours later he finds himself in a marketplace talking with people there (it's not difficult; English has become the universal language) and they seem so disconcertingly like folks back home in Springfield or Omaha. Here are the same interests and concerns — about family, prices, weather, jobs, housing, threats of war — that at first he may feel a little let down.

But, in my case at least, that initial sense of disappointment was soon supplanted by an exhilarating feeling of confirmation. All my life I have staunchly believed in what for want of a better phrase we call the brotherhood of man. And my travels around the world have been a shining vindication of that belief. They have proved what I have thought in my mind and felt in my heart about the essential oneness of the human race.

It really is true: when you get down beneath the surface layer of outward appearance and native custom, human beings are remarkably alike. In different parts of the world people may dress and sometimes look a bit differently. Yet underneath, anatomically, biologically, psychologically, we are all virtually the same. When a man recognizes this esential sameness, this universal oneness, when he looks upon the people he meets, not as strangers but as potential friends and comrades, life's journey becomes a cheerful progression and not a forced march.

As I have said, my travels around the world have been such an edifying and expansive experience for me more because of the people I have met than the places I have been. It was years ago that I stood witness as an intrepid old Frenchman down in Haiti defied the then-dictator "Papa Doc" Duvalier and risked his life to help an injured native who was out of favor with the government. From that old man, I learned a valorous lesson in the meaning of courage.

I remember long conversations under South Pacific

stars with a brilliant Chinese woman named Myra Wong. We were on a steamer bound from Manila for Hong Kong. The ancient wisdom of the Orient illumined her words as she taught me a priceless lesson in the meaning of human relationships and why we must build stronger, more durable bridges between East and West.

I remember an old innkeeper somewhere in the back country of northern India who took care of me when I was acutely sick. He did not know me at all, he had no obligation to this stranger with whom he could scarcely converse, yet he gently showed me the meaning of the Good Samaritan parable as I had never really understood it before.

And I remember sitting up most of a summer night in Oslo and talking with a young Norwegian diplomat, just returned from service with the United Nations, who helped me realize more clearly than ever why from now on we **must** have one world or we will not have any world. My Scandinavian friend quoted a sentence from Tom Paine I was so familiar with we recited it together: "My country is the world, and my religion is to do good."

If in a few words I had to summarize what I have learned from my global wanderings, I think I would say this. I have learned that life is our father; that earth is our mother; that all men and women are our brothers and sisters; that religions are many, but religion is one; and that there is only one race — the human race.

The Last and Greatest
Frontier of All

Ask almost any intelligent person these days what he or she thinks the last great frontier of human investigation will be, and the answer you are likely to get is, the exploration of outer space. Something that has always seemed a preposterous dream is rapidly becoming an almost mundane reality, what with our space labs, moon landings, soon-to-come planetary landings, speed-of-light radio signals and rockets streaking off to the far corners of the cosmos. Surely space and all its mysteries is the last frontier.

Yet perhaps not. For there is another cosmos that involves not the vastnesses of outer space, but the quite as stange reaches of inner space, of that **terra incognita** that lies within the human soul and psyche. It may well be that the last and greatest frontier of all is the one that runs through the minds and hearts of us earthlings.

Scholars have long been bemused by the fact that we had discovered a remarkable deal about our universe ages before we learned very much about ourselves. Thousands of years ago the early Chinese, Babylonians, Egyptians, Greeks and, later, Mayans knew a surprising lot about astronomy. Accurately they predicted eclipses and determined the positions and movements of stars. Aristarchus, a Greek astronomer, even had the effrontery to propose that the earth is round and that in company with the other planets it revolves about the sun. For centuries now people have known what makes the earth go around, but only today are we developing some fair notion of what makes us go around.

So it may be that the next and, in terms of its implications for our race, perhaps our greatest exploratory adventure will be one that takes us down into hidden, often forbidden, regions where we develop a deeper, more revealing understanding of human behavior, nature and potential. And then, wiser and emboldened, we will apply what we have learned to the betterment of mankind and the advancement of the human enterprise. We will do this, let us fervently pray, not in any doctrinaire, authoritarian fashion, but in the way that understanding parents and democratic societies educate and civilize.

This is certainly not to suggest that our ancestors had little insight into or understanding of the human condition. Of course they had. But that intelligence had never been freed of theological intrusion, nor had it been systematized, shaped into theories and used for therapeutic purposes.

Now, however, during the eight decades of this century we have learned prodigiously more about us mortals that we had ever known before: about why we love, hate, hope, fear, fight, care, worship, sacrifice and, in general, why, for better or worse, we do whatever we do. Before our time, the Human Reclamation and Improvement Project was largely dependent on insight, common sense, haphazardly observed experience and accumulated wisdom. Not at all a bad assortment of tools to work with! But The Project suffered from the same deficiencies that restricted science: lack of objectivity, experimentation, verifiable results, interchange of information, technological know-how and, most of all, simply from lack of a wide-open, no-fences field of inquiry.

Today the fences are down and the field is virtually unlimited. The challenge now is to move across new frontiers and use our so-recently gained psychical and physical knowledge to accelerate the civilizing process. Consider this proposition: in a meliorist, maturational sense and from a salvationist point of view, isn't it reasonable to assume that what we have lately been learning about people is more promising than what we have been learning about things (whether "things" be construed as computerization, electromagnetism, quantum, "black holes," or whatever).

It is not in scientific achievements, however impressive, or in political systems, however effective, that our destiny lies, but rather in the cultivation of the human potential and the transformation, if not from animal to angel, at least from what we now are to what conceivably we might be. To blast off into space and reveal the secrets of Mars will be a Promethean feat indeed. But to cross a closer frontier and explore, however partially and imperfectly, the mysteries of the human psyche and soul may be the most revelatory space flight of all. Even if the space is not outer but inner . . .

Conversation With a Tree

If the title of this piece sounds to you like no more than a bit of whimsy, I must gently disabuse you. And I have the historical record to support me. The arboreal fact is that for centuries past in many parts of the world trees have been worshipped and have been regarded as possessing all sorts of magical and mystical properties.

In fact, sacred trees seem to have grown abundantly almost everywhere. On the **Beagle's** pioneering voyage, Darwin discovered and wrote about several of them. In North America, Europe, Asia, Africa he would have done as well. Often there is believed to be an organic connection, akin to a blood relationship, between people and their holy trees.

Perhaps the best known example of tree worship is provided by the Druids who were a sort of priestly class among the ancient inhabitants of Great Britain and Gaul. The Druids regarded the oak as being specially sacred. They believed that on select occasions oak trees spoke to them. (Hence, in case you have wondered, "Conversation With a Tree").

I do not go quite as far as two or our most respected sages, Plutarch and Aristotle, who maintained that trees have passions and perceptions. And, unlike the Druids, I have never had an oak tree speak to me. Although I swear that on certain enchanted evenings the soughing in the wind in one of our pines at Maple Juice Cove has tried to tell me something.

After all, communication takes various forms and, as I ponder the matter, I realize how many lessons I have learned from our woodsy friends. For example, this is the first time I have spoken in defence of intolerance (but then this is a pretty odd piece). What I have in mind is that most flowers, ferns, shrubs are tolerant things; they can tolerate a good deal of shadow and shade. But a great redwood or Norway pine makes no such concession. It insists upon thrusting straight up into the sunlight and it lives up there with a calm composure the gods must envy.

The trouble with so many of us is that, like the ferns and the huckleberry bushes, we are too tolerant. We are content to grow in the shade; we adjust to our environment without a struggle; we settle for life on the easiest terms. Like a great tree, we need to grow up and up and up to where the air is freer and the light is brighter.

Having just pronounced in favor of intolerance, I must now compound the felony by assuming a kind of anti-democratic stance. About a tall and stately tree there is something lordly and imperial as it stands forth against the sky. No wonder our ancestors worshipped trees. Few kings have seemed as kingly as the monarchs of the forest.

When I wander through John Muir's redwood wonderland in California, I am suffused with a sense of nobility, a supernal awareness that life is big and splendid and made of heroic stuff. In a different yet compatible way, I am equally animated when I walk down the main aisle of Westminster Abbey, or listen to the last movement of Sibelius' Second Symphony, or view Michelangelo's sublime creations in Florence or Rome. Great trees remind a democratic society not to forget the grandeur, glory and nobility of life.

Another quality I love about our forest friends, if you don't mind an oxymoron, is their comparative immortality. Of course no tree lives forever, but, on the few occasions when we permit them to, they can survive for centuries. Redwoods again. 2000 years old! It was Donald Culross Peattie who reminded us that some of those giants span the whole panorama of Christian history. As they were sprouting, Jesus was born in Bethlehem.

In a highly mobile society such as ours where few things seem permanent any more, people are rootless and change is the name of the game, the abiding permanence of great trees is a serenely restful and reassuring reality.

And one thing more: what I would simply call their peacefulness. Anybody who has not wandered at will through a solitary woods, the sense that of an outdoors cathedral whose choristers are the birds, whose light filters fitfully through green leaves above and whose incense is the pungency of the earth beneath, has never learned what tranquillity really means. Maybe our not so primitive ancestors were wiser than we think to have identified trees so intimately with religion.

Here's a suggestion from them to us: When the persisting life problems of getting and giving, of living and loving become too vexatious, why not forget about counselors and counseling and all other such intermediation and go out and just have a nice quiet talk with a tree . . .

On Doing One's Duty

A major problem with the subject of this book is that its focus tends to be a personal one. And that's only natural. After all, the task of mining life's riches, and of making sure they are the right sort of capital, is pretty much up to you and me. No one else can live our lives for us, and no one else can get for us what there is wisely to be gained.

But in the process never for a moment should we forget that we are social creatures with innumerable social responsibilities and that the foremost obligation of our lives is not so much a personal as a social one. Regrettably, we and our contemporaries do forget more than we care to realize.

From a moral and ethical point of view, the twentieth century has been a highly relativistic and laissez-faire period. Not only have we imposed few moral and ethical standards on our children, but in many cases we have not even known what such standards might be. This is to say that millions of us are moral illiterates.

For instance, many of us do not realize that a price we must pay for enriching and ennobling our life's experience is a social price. This is not a word we use very much these days, but the fact remains that all of us have an imperative social **duty**. My dictionary defines duty simply as "a thing a person ought to do." That's about as clear as a definition can be, but it is also as fundamental.

Perhaps we moderns shy away from this concept because it has so often been abused in the past. Think of all the weary times people have been told they must do their duty to their chieftan or their king or even their God — when there did not seem to be any sane reason for doing so. Never mind, don't ask questions: just do your duty.

Tennyson's "The Charge of the Light Brigade" is remembered, not because it is notable poetry, which it is not, but because it so dramatically describes a monstrous, and true life, perversion of duty. Although they knew the order was an insane mistake and meant the brigade's annihilation, riding in perfect order, 600 men charged "into the valley of death" and were blown to a holocaust of bloody bits. An appalling example of how its devotion to duty has sometimes betrayed mankind.

By contrast, now see what duty can and should mean in the civilized community. The obligation is spelled out plainly and imperishably in the first five books of the Old Testament. What it says in effect is this: You shall look after the needs of the widowed and the fatherless. You shall attend the afflicted. You shall see to the wants of the stranger who is within your gates. And so on. Why shall you do all this? Setting aside questions of love, compassion and just plain human decency, the answer is, **because it is your duty**.

These injunctions were promulgated and accepted by the Children of Israel over 2500 years ago, yet the passing centuries have not improved upon them. What they represent, both in substance and spirit, has been the moral, social and religious foundation of Western civilization. The individual is important. Of course. Supremely so. Let no one question this. Yet on occasion he or she has certain duties and obligations that transcend all personal considerations. For them, when they justify the price, good men and women are willing to live — and die. Again, why? And again we can answer most simply, and come nearest the mark, by saying, because it is their duty.

Here in recent times one of America's most respected philosophers Josiah Royce talked about duty as loyalty and said: "The value of life lies not in what individuals get out of it, but in the supreme and super-individual value of loyalty. Loyalty, the devotion of the self to the interests of the community, is indeed the form which the highest life of humanity must take. Without loyalty, there is no salvation. The detached individual is an essentially lost being."

Or consider these words of H.C. Trumbull, "All that any one of us has to do in this world is his simple duty. An archangel could not do more to advantage."

Or these:

Question — "Am I my brother's keeper?"

Answer — "Yes!"

On Being Lost in the Fog

It was a crisp New England afternoon aflame in late September colors — the kind pilgrims come from all over the country to learn what chromatics really means — and Isabel and I were pointed east on a five-day outing through the idyllic cruising waters of Penobscot Bay. About four o'clock, we noticed what appeared to be fog banks building up ahead of us, and prudently we opted to head for shelter. Our choice was Pulpit Harbor on North Haven Island. Both harbor and island look as though they had been expressly designed for picture calendar and postcard reproduction, and that is where you have seen them a hundred times.

Something else that would impress you, if you have never experienced it, is the dismaying swiftness with which fog can close in. Before it grew too thick, we picked up the whistle buoy near Robinson Rock and that confirmed our course. Now it was a race — albeit a frustratingly slow and cautious one — between us and the fog. Here again, in its density and opacity, you have to be swallowed up by a Down East fog before you have any real sense of what one is like. Enveloped by it, you can see nothing at all except a few feet of boat. In the incautious event that you do not have a compass and if wind and tide have been moving your craft, as they have been, there is no way you can tell which is north, south, east or west. For all the good they do, you may as well close your eyes — and open your ears and other senses to whatever feeble messages they may transmit.

It was that sort of fog that was rolling in fast. Just as it completely engulfed us, dimly we caught a glimpse of the most beautiful sight in the world, Pulpit Rock! The narrow entrance to Pulpit Harbor is marked by a large boulder at the end of a ledge, and a vessel works its way around the rock and into the shelter of the harbor. By feel, by guess and by God, that is what we did. Isabel and I still speak of the flood of relief that swept over us like a Bay of Fundy tide as the anchor took hold. Now, all of a sudden, the safety and security of the harbor transformed the fog from lowering menace into an innocuous kind of drifting nacreous beauty.

Sitting on deck in that eerie translucent light, it occurred to me that, as part of their training, perhaps all psychologists and psychiatrists should be left at sea for a few hours in a small boat without a compass in a thick Down East fog. As professionals, they frequently deal with patients who are confused, disoriented, lost. Well, believe me, nothing would nurture a keener sense of empathy on the part of doctor for patient than such an experience!

I also thought of some words I had set down a few months earlier when another zero-zero fog had swallowed up our house back at Maple Juice Cove. There in that all-enveloping murk and mist I had written this:

* * * * * * * * *

Only a few minutes ago ours was a shining, bright, refulgent world, the air so transparently clear I could count branches on trees across the cove and gulls wheeling far out toward the open sea.

But now the fog has come — from where? from what malevolent source? — and so swiftly too, cloud after cloud rolling in like some dark threat made tangible, implacably advancing to consume and destroy. Now the sun, trees, gulls, even the sea itself have disappeared and there is only this devouring damp grayness drifting into one's eyes, nose, soul. Only the disorienting nothingness of the fog and a silence like the day after the end of the world. Only this sense of strangeness, emptiness, lostness as though Hope had died and the phantom fog were the only reality.

And yet, when I compel my mind to admit the fact, I know that beyond this insubstantial vapor the trees still staunchly guard our quiet cove, the gulls still wheel and soar, the sun still shines exultantly. It is a good thing for a man to force his mind in such a way for fog, mystery, the unknown can sweep in suddenly from some fantastic sea and seem to consume all things both real and dear.

Yet a cloud passing across the sun is . . . a cloud passing across the sun, no more than that. It is a good thing to remember the insubstantiality, the temporary and ephemeral nature of the fog. And to remember too that fog is not some alien force from some inimical other world, but simply a part of the natural reality whose more familiar aspects are trees, birds, rolling sea and shining sun.

* * * * * * * * * *

Dare to be Different!

Cave men and women disappeared from this planet millenia ago. Or so the anthropologists tell us. The only trouble with our scientific friends is that they define "cave" in too limited a way. If they would look around the late twentieth century scene, they might not be so cocksure about who disappeared when.

For the unsettling fact is that **Homo neanderthalensis** still has more than a few descendants around and about. They may not live in a hollow in the earth, but they do dwell in a place where little light shines. They live there because they are frightened creatures. What are they frightened of? Differences! So intimidated are they by deviation and divergence that they spin out their pallid lives knowing only one church, one small group of people indistinguishable from themselves, one meager, colorless way of life. To change the image a bit, they are like men and women dwelling in a sparse, dark valley who have never troubled to climb the nearby mountain and see the splendor of sunrise and sunset and all the glories of the world.

That is a grandeur best known by those stout souls who have learned to enjoy and revel in the unending richness and variety of life. These are they who truly possess the world for all its peoples, places and pleasures are theirs to relish and profit by. Every man or woman is their friend, or potentially so; every altar is theirs to kneel at and be heartened by; every country and culture is theirs to delight in and learn from. This world of ours is a treasure chest unbounded, but only to those who can see and appreciate its treasures.

Ever since I first visited it, I have felt that Hong Kong may be the most fascinating city on earth, not because of its unparalleled setting, but simply because of the swarming, multifarious variety of its life with every kind of color, creed and culture all mixed up in our closest approach to a truly global melting pot. How much more bracing and ebullient life would be if we had more cities like Hong Kong!

That Frenchman who when somebody mentioned the difference between the sexes cried out **Vive la différence!** was as wise a man as he was a wit. Long live the precious differences, peculiarities, idiosyncrasies that give our lives so much of their flavor and pungency. Long live Emerson's non-conformism and Thoreau's prickly individualism. Long live all men and women who have the courage to be themselves, even if they fit no particular pattern by so being, and who have the strength of character to help their children develop fully and freely, unhampered by the senseless customs and conventions that so often repress and constrict young life.

Learned Hand, who was one of this country's most esteemed judges and jurists, once warned, "Our dangers, it seems to me, are not from the outrageous but from the conforming; not from those who rarely and under the lurid glare of obloquy upset our moral complaisance, or shock us with unaccustomed conduct, but from those, the mass of us, who take their virtues and their tastes, like their shirts and their furniture, from the limited patterns which the market offers."

We live today in a world that enjoys a lovely mix of cast and color: ebony black, dusky black, sepia, ocher, honey, **café au lait** and a rich variety of other browns and yellows, as well, of course, as a color scale ranging from fish-belly white to, ironically, a much sought-after sun-tan bronze. As the centuries wear on, this palette of human hues will probably be reduced to a single all-pervading color, just as our various cultures may meld and flow into one ubiquitous monotony. I must say I find the prospect a melancholy one. Black and white are the minimum, the rainbow of the spectrum is the maximum. I prefer rainbows . . .

Far from fearing differences, we should delight in them for they are what make life colorful, zestful, variegated, exciting. They are a principal means by which we learn fresh and, presumably, better ways of doing things. They are, in fact, one of the root secrets of evolution for this is the way life advances — by developing new and different forms and species.

The man or woman who is free of the spurious security that conformity affords; who is confident enough to face up to and enjoy the invigorating differences between peoples, religions, customs and ideas; and who is capable of learning from the enlightening experiences they provide — here is a human being much to be envied. For to him or her life may be busy, and occasionally dizzy!, but it will never be flat or insipid. It will always be richly and rousingly worth living!

Life as Discipline

Discipline. It's not a word we hear much these days and one we probably like even less. The connotations are grim. It rings with a jackboot, lock-up, crack-the-whip sound.

Too bad. Much too bad. For the obdurate fact is that most of the time — with a good many obvious exceptions — you and I get what we work for in this world. Or, to sharpen the point a little, we get what we **discipline** ourselves for.

For example, all of us would like to be reasonably successful in life. But so often the price of success is discipline. As Havelock Ellis knew, "For the artist life is always discipline." It is, at least at first, the hard, dull, monotonous business of forcing ourselves to do the same thing over and over and over again until slowly we develop the skills and proficiencies we want and need. One of the endless ironies of our human lot is that we tend to think of discipline in terms of punishment when we ought to think of it in terms of reward.

Occasionally one meets a person who seems to have hit the jackpot when brains, personality and talent were passed out. He or she is one of those lucky aberrations that happens every now and then, a man or woman who was born at the top of the ladder and didn't have painstakingly to climb up a series of steps marked discipline and development.

But the great majority of us are not that fortunate.

We have to take this imperfect instrument which is our mind and body and slowly train and develop it. All of which can be subsumed under one word, discipline. Most of the successful artists, scientists, business men and women — in fact, it seems safe to say, most of the successful people in the world today — have gotten where they are because they trained themselves, which is to say, they disciplined themselves, to do the job.

One of our common misconceptions lies in assuming that discipline makes life harder, more monnotonous, less appealing. Actually, the reverse is true. The well-disciplined individual is a man or woman who finds life easier, smoother, less complicated than most of us do. This is so because almost automatically he performs the manifold small tasks and duties that often bother the rest of us so much. The difference between the well-disciplined person and the average person is the difference between a smoothly-running, well-lubricated machine and one that is a little out of line whose gears are beginning to grind.

By all means, let us also note that the reward of discipline is likely to be not only success, but what may be even more meaningful in a deep interior sense, a glowing awareness of pride and satisfaction. The climber who finally reaches the top of the mountain receives more rewards than he may have expected.

Just because he was such a practical, commonsensical fellow, even at an early age Benjamin Franklin appreciated the economies and efficiencies of discipline. When he was in his early twenties, Franklin and another young man set out to learn Italian. At the same time they were also beginning to play chess. Before long they were just playing chess and ignoring their study. But Franklin soon realized what was happening and refused to play any longer unless it was agreed that the loser should translate 50 pages of Italian before the game was resumed. As luck would have it, the two men were fairly evenly matched, and, as Franklin later said, they beat each other into a knowledge of Italian.

The man or woman who appreciates the uses and values of discipline, as Franklin did, has discovered the great secret of authority — of authority over himself. The noted American biologist Edwin Grant Conklin agreed; he said, "The essence of all education is self discovery and self-control." The general assumption is that education is basically a matter of learning lots and lots about more and more.

But education is equally a matter of discipline and self-mastery. After years of arduous graduate study, the young doctor and lawyer know — they have to know — a staggering amount about their respective fields. Yet all that abundance of information and knowledge means little unless they have also developed adequate control — of ideas, skills, techniques, mental processes . . . and of themselves. Control of his knowledge and himself is as crucial to the medical doctor as it is to the airline pilot.

The most important, and the most difficult, thing to control in this world is not other people; it is oneself. And beyond all other elements, the secret of that control is discipline. As the Buddha said, "The wise who control their body, who control their tongue, the wise who control their mind, are indeed well controlled."

To Reach, or Not to Reach, For a Star

These unsettling and confusing days we are often told, especially in life adjustment courses and articles on popular psychology, that we ought to set reasonable goals for ourselves we have some fair chance of achieving. We are advised that a lot of our anxiety and discontent results because we are trying to attain things beyond our grasp or positions that most of us will never reach. What we should do, therefore, is accept our limitations and try not to extend ourselves too far beyond them. After all, one of the first commandments of good mental health is to accept ourselves as we really are and not as we fancifully might like to be.

On the other hand, we find what seems to be an exactly opposite kind of advice. For centuries now philosophy and religion have urged us to over-extend and outdo ourselves, to set goals as high as the stars, to attempt to realize the impossible dream. Said Michelangelo, "God grant that I may always desire more than I can accomplish." Said Emerson. "Hitch your wagon to a star." Said William Blake, "Great things are done when men and mountains meet; this is not done by jostling in the street."

Now here are two almost diametrically opposite kinds of advice that concern us all in a weighty way. Should we reach or not reach for a star? Confusing, perhaps, but not as contradictory as it may seem. Can't we resolve the dilemma along these lines. Yes, the fact is inescapable: all of us have our own particular, personal limitations about which we will probably never be able to do very much. It is in these restricted areas that we had better set relatively easy, not Everest-high goals for ourselves.

Example. Although I love to listen to music, I have little aptitude for creating it. If I were to take the time, I could probably learn to play the piano, but there is paltry reason to believe that I could ever play it very well. Conclusion: Stick to "Chopsticks"; eschew Chopin.

Example. Here is a young man who has a keen interest in science. The problem is: average intelligence. There is no indication that he could do advanced scientific work. He would have to make a real effort to get and keep a job as a lab assistant. Perhaps that should be his goal.

Example. Consider this family that has never managed money well and in which both parents have frequently moved from job to job. They had better not dream of estates in Florida, 40-foot yachts or any other such delectable fantasies. A small cottage on a nearby lake may be as much as they should aspire to.

Now please note that none of these dreams is a small one — for the people involved. Actually, they are good-sized ones, comparatively speaking. But they are dreams that we of modest prospect would have some reasonable chance of attaining. And, after all, the satisfactions we find in life are not so much determined by the size of our goals as by our qualifications for achievement, by the vigorous effort we make to achieve and, if it may be, by the sweet taste of success. To know we have what it takes is the real reward, and it doesn't make much difference whether we have been bucking for section foreman or president of the company.

Now let's work the other side of the street for a few minutes. Repeatedly we have recognized that each of us has his or her own personal skills and abilities. It is in these areas of our special aptitude that we ought to take off the brakes, step on the gas and attempt to climb some high hills — at least, high for us. I may not be able to play a piano, but I can play a typewriter. Moral: write. You may not care much for housekeeping and cooking, but you love to paint. So — paint.

The full, free exercise of what talents we do have is going to afford us a gratifying measure of satisfaction — and surprise. We may not reach a star, but we might touch one of the smaller asteroids. In fact, this is the way much of the world's progress has been made: by men and women who reached further than they ever thought they could. With their new inventions, theories, techniques or discoveries, they surprised the world. But between you and me, I'll bet they were the most surprised of all.

The person who has never made this attempt to extend, or even over-extend, himself is much to be pitied for he has never discovered the exceptional stuff that is in him or gotten as much as he might and could and should get out of life. Stars have many uses, as any astronomer, navigator or poet will tell you. But what finer purpose can they serve than to be the object of our reaching, and yearning, and, just possibly, touching . . .

"The Simple Little Things of Life"

It was a long time ago, and yet through all the intervening years I have never forgotten the old man's advice. I couldn't have been more than 12 years old; he was in his late 70s. We were fishing one early morning on one of the most beautiful lakes in northern Minnesota. Fishing was what he loved to do more than anything in the world.

After awhile he looked around — at the incredibly clear blue water and the even bluer sky and the black green of pine against the shore and the sunlight dancing all about us — and he said, "It's good, isn't it?"

And then he said — and this is what I have never forgotten — "You know, boy, it's the simple little things of life that are so often the best. Things like fishing, and just being in the sun, and listening to bird calls, and the way the pine smells on a hot summer day. I'd rather be right here in this boat than anywhere else on earth."

That was quite a long speech for him, so he stopped and went back to his fishing.

"The simple, little things of life . . ." How often through the years I have remembered his words. I have remembered them because experience has taught me the wisdom of them. They go a long way toward explaining a basic secret of human happiness. Certainly they do much to explain why wealth, material possessions, worldly goods, even fame and acclaim are no guarantee of happiness. Wise men have always told us this, but most of us have trouble understanding or really believing them.

If you are one of the skeptics, I would suggest you spend a little time with a few of the ancients like Epictetus or Marcus Aurelius or Seneca, or some of our latter-day writers like Emerson and Thoreau, or John Burroughs and John Muir. They may open your eyes — and refresh your spirit.

No, my old fisherman friend was right. Money and the things that money buys can't really speak to the soul as sunlight and bird calls and wind in the pines do. Before we can know any deeper kind of happiness, we have to go beyond creature comforts and material satisfactions to things that touch our hearts and spirits.

They don't have to be big things. In fact, big things often get in the way. But they have to be real . . . basic . . . elemental things. They have to make a man be able to speak from the depths of his being, as my old friend did, and say, "It's good, isn't it?"

Two of the most famous lines in English poetry are from a poem by William Blake. Said he,

> "To see the world in a grain of sand
> And heaven in a wild flower."

That's the trick: to be able to find all sorts of beauty and meaning in something as simple as a grain of sand or a wild flower. My old fishing companion was no poet or philosopher, yet he thought and spoke like both.

One of the reasons I am such a confirmed believer in the reading of good biography is that it provides so many practical, profitable lessons. Time and again we learn that periodically even the great and famous have to get away from it all — from the spectacle and fanfare and parade — and go off by themselves for awhile, preferably to some modest place in the woods or by the seashore.

There they find rest and recuperation. They renew their perspective. And in the simple, little things of life they rediscover so many of the essential meanings of life. They learn all over again that even the mightiest nations and empires eventually decline, that wealth and power dissipate and "the captains and the kings depart." But the natural, elemental things of life — sunrise, rainfall, spring and autumn, summer and winter, birth and death — these go on and on and on. And from this lesson, the great, if they are truly great, and the wise, if they are truly wise, learn humility and patience.

Great and wise persons through the centuries have made this pilgrimage, away from all the pomp and pageantry of state to the fundamentals of life. When they do, they learn again what one might call the secret of simplicity.

I first learned the secret on a perfect summer day in a little fishing boat long ago in the heart of the Minnesota woods.

"Sow a Habit"

One of the marvels of the twentieth century is a technique we have developed for vastly speeding up work: we call it automation. The term is a combination of two words, automatic operation, and that pretty well tells the story. Isn't it wonderful!, we exclaim. Who would have thought it.

Who? Wise men and women through the centuries have thought it. Only they used another word. They called it — habit. And they not only used it, they also did what we should always do with such words, they applied it. With Americans of an earlier day, few items stood higher on their list of essentials than good habit formation. And like Prussian drillmasters, they hassled and harried their children until they too were intensely habit-conscious.

Unfortunately for us, their latter-day indolent progeny, tradition seems to have worn distressingly thin. Habit may well be one of the many casualties of this discipline-shy modern world. We do not place anywhere near as much emphasis as our forbears did on the desirability of cultivating good habits and thereby improving the quality of our lives. And most of us parents do not make the effort fathers and mothers once made to inculcate good habit patterns as a natural, routine practice in the upbringing of our children. This is a lamentable failure on our part for there are few worthier services we could render them. As G.D. Boardman has said, "Sow an act, and you reap a habit; sow a habit, and you reap a character; sow a character, and you reap a destiny."

We may as well recognize, however, that the cultivation of good habits takes a bit of doing, particularly where we adults are concerned. This is so for the reason that we have grown a bit stiff in the psychological joints; we have developed considerable built-in resistance to change. Laziness, tardiness, sloppiness, inattention, procrastination are the sort of characteristics many of us have formed during a lifetime, and they are not going to be altered quickly. They have become almost as much a part of us as the way we walk or talk.

But then nobody has said that they can change or have to be changed overnight. "A habit cannot be tossed out a window," Mark Twain correctly observed; "it must be coaxed down the stairs one step at a time." At the start, a little concentrated daily attention will suffice. Then as the pace is increased and new habits are formed, we will automatically adjust ourselves to the new and better way of doing things.

As simply as anyone could, the Greek Stoic philosopher Epictetus two millenia ago described the process of habit formation. Said he, "Every habit is preserved and increased by corresponding actions; as the habit of walking, by walking; of running, by running. If you would be a reader, read; if a writer, write. After sitting still for ten days, get up and attempt to take a long walk, and you will find how your legs are weakened. Whatever you would make habitual, practice it; and if you would not make a thing habitual, do not practice it, but habituate yourself to something else."

As Epictetus recognized, the word "automatic" is the secret where habit is concerned. Most habits are automatic; we do certain things without even realizing we are doing them. Habit thus quickly becomes a self-acting device for the improvement and betterment of human beings. William James called it "the enormous flywheel of society." He said, "The great thing is to make our nervous system our ally instead of our enemy." He then went on to point out that many people waste much of their time trying to make decisions about matters that ought to be so ingrained as practically not to exist for their consciousness at all.

We present-day Americans are much impressed by what has been done with automation. Look at an ad for a new house and it will proudly feature the many "labor-saving" devices the house contains. It never occurs to us that the best labor-saving "device" of all is a human being who has taken much of the drudgery, repetition and unnecessary effort out of life by virtue of a simple mechanism called habit.

"Cultivate good habits" may sound like an old-fashioned copybook maxim. But it is still unbeatable advice on the felicitous subject of getting more out of life. If it is true that people are "walking bundles of habit," then it follows that few things in our lives are more important than good habit formation. Now there's one habit that's really worth getting into!

The Animal Kingdom

If you were a contestant on one of TV's ubiquitous game shows and were asked the following question, I'll bet the show's $25,000 jackpot you'd give the wrong answer. Question: Among the larger animals on this planet, which is the most numerous species? Your probable answer: cattle, or hogs, or sheep. Wrong (or **gong!**) Correct answer: people. There are today almost five billion human beings crowding the earth, but you have to go all the way down the scale to creatures the size of squirrels and rabbits to find other species that are numbered by the thousands of millions.

Unfortunately, it is scarcely necessary to add that the larger wild animals like lions, tigers, bears, bison, elephants have been virtually eliminated. The staggering fact is that the human population is now greater than that of all the large animals combined. Since horses have little utilitarian value today, wool is becoming increasingly unnecessary, and plant food or protein is rapidly going to replace animal food, we are faced with the incredible prospect of a world in which there are practically no large animals left, other than us Hominids.

One's initial reaction to this news must certainly be surprise, even shock. But once the surprise has worn off, do we simply shrug our shoulders and say, Well, that's just another price we have to pay for progress. To think in such unfeeling, cavalier terms would be to demonstrate how far we have moved from our evolutionary past, forgetting untold millions of years of common life with the animal kingdom. We like to talk these days about "extended families." Yet how can we be so insensitive as not to mourn the passing of that zoological family with which we have lived, mostly in harmony, since we were an indistinguishable part of it ourselves? Indeed, something of what we are and have been is passing too. Elsewhere, we have talked about the shameful calamities that have stained our century's history: world wars, the Holocaust, the nuclear threat. To that Doomsday day list we should add: the rapid decline and reduction to zoo status of the animal kingdom.

What we late twentieth century types do not realize is that up until only a handful of decades ago our forebears lived in a close, communal, almost symbiotic relationship with the animals. Prior to a hundred years ago, most Americans were farmers. They did not have to do with machines, they had to do with animals. What is more it was a warm, vital, sensate relationship. Animals may not be human, but they are living, responsive creatures. There is all the difference in the universe between them and a rock or a piece of steel. They call forth responses and stimulate a flesh-and-blood feeling as no machines can ever do.

Modern civilization is a dead civilization to the extent that there are virtually no animals in it. It is all machinery and electricity and hi-tech incomprehensibles. So we have to ask this question: in such a soulless world, what is going to happen to the human soul? I use this word "soul" advisedly because I have in mind a fascinating controversy that broke out in Europe during the seventeenth century. At issue was the question of whether animals have souls. Taking the negative was the leading French philosopher of the day, Descartes. Presumably he had never heard a whale sing or a dolphin click, and he based his argument on the faculty of speech and symbolic language.

I am happy to report that M. Descartes got his comeuppance. By way of rebuttal, another eminent philosopher, Leibnitz, contended that not only do animals have souls, but that man is not essentially different from all other forms of life. We are all part of a wondrous cosmic life force. It was an attitude not unlike Albert Schweitzer's and his reverence-for-life principle.

Well, the question of soul, and of what meaning the word may have, aside for the moment, can't we at least agree with Schweitzer about the sanctity of life, whether animal or human. The bottom line would seem to be this: that our time-beyond-counting association with the animals has given us a fellow-and-family feeling we simply cannot experience in any other way. If we anthropoids are going to get as much out of life as we can and should, all signals indicate that, before it is too late, we had better open our arms and hearts and get better acquainted with our relatives . . You might call it a family reunion . . .

Life Does Go On

When I was a boy I spent most of my summers up in the beautiful lake country of northern Minnesota. Back in those days forest fires ravaged that wilderness land a good deal more than they do now. Many times in my youth I saw areas where for miles around fire had destroyed virtually every living thing, leaving only a sickening sense of ruin and devastation. Looking upon them, I had a dreadful sense of finality, as though this were the end, as though the land had been despoiled forever.

Yet 20 years after those boyhood vacations of mine, I visited northern Minnesota again. It was a heartening, and surprising, experience. To this day I remember how astonished I was to see how quickly the forest had returned. Now the land was green once more; there were sizeable stands of balsam, pine and birch almost everywhere. Except for the absence of any really large trees, one would scarcely know that forest fires had so recently raged there. And I thought to myself, Despite all the terrible things that can happen to it — fire, flood, famine, drought, earthquake — somehow or other, life does go on. It was a wonderfully bracing thought.

A good many more years went by, and this time my parents had a summer home deep in the woods of northern Massachusetts. Here again forests surrounded the place; beyond our open fields, huge trees reached in every direction. Yet when I wandered through those woods, I would discover a curious thing. Far back in what seemed to be virgin forest, I would suddenly come upon an old stone fence, fallen to ruin and almost hidden by the undergrowth — the sort of thing Robert Frost liked to write about.

The more I worked my way through the woods, the more fences I found. Gradually it dawned on me that one or two hundred years before, all this had been open country. Farming country. These had been open fields from which our rugged New England ancestors had wrested a hardy living. But when the far-reaching, fertile Western lands opened up, they found it no longer worth the effort. So some farmers stopped trying, and others moved away. And gradually, but quickly, surprisingly quickly, the forest moved back and took over again. Plants, bushes, trees reclaimed the land, and now, a century or two later, a man would never know that this had once been open country. He would never know, that is, except for the tell-tale fences and an occasional cellar hole filled with the moldering accretions of time. Again I would think how quickly nature reasserts herself. Once more, it's the old, indomitable story. Somehow or other, life does go on.

This simple sustaining truth I have learned in the woods of Minnesota and Massachusetts, as I have also learned on the Maine coast and the Arizona desert, is a reassuring one for you and me to remember. For in all our lives there are going to be dark, depressive times when it looks as though we have finally come to the end of the road. The future is closed. There is no hope. The sign says stop. Life simply can't go any farther.

Well, we may feel this defeatist way. We may even

have reason to feel this way. But the indisputable fact remains that we are wrong. Because there is always an answer, a way out. Somehow or other, life does go on. Just look, if you please, at the record.

Through uncountable eons of time, from a far, dim day when salt waters covered the earth and a spirit of creation moved restlessly upon it; from that unimaginable day to this, a miracle has slowly, ever slowly, been unfolding upon this planet. That miracle is **Life**! It is life triumphant and irresistible!

To read the story of life, from its microsopic origins several billion years ago, through the long epochs of geologic change, through the eternity of sea-like beginnings, and the age of the reptiles, and of the mammals, and, beginning a million years ago, of the anthropoids, culminating only yesterday in the emergence of **Homo sapiens**, or you and me, the highest form (we like to think) of evolutionary development to date — I say, to read this story is to feel a sense of resilience and reassurance beyond compare. For nothing, **nothing** has been able to stop the onward, upward movement of life. No disaster, no cataclysm, not even the old adversary death has been able to halt the forward sweep of life victorious.

Now if that isn't a success story, if it isn't the most inspiring single certainty about this little planet of ours, you tell me what is. Call it an **élan vital** . . . creative force . . . God . . . it is a wonderous living reality we can see and sense in the ageless, indestructible world of nature all about us. It is a lesson full of four billion years of promise and affirmation, and it is told in four simple words — life does go on.

It Is Not Only the Blind
Who Cannot See

In my travels around the world, I have had a host
of memorable experiences. One of them occurred on
a glorious summer day back when the century was a
little younger and so was I. I was taking my first boat
trip down the Rhine River in Germany. Towering above
the heights on both sides of the water were fairytale
castles. Perched up there hundreds of feet above our
heads, they were breathtaking sights. I almost expected
knights in shining armor to come marching out of them
and fair maidens to throw roses from the balconies.

Tumbling down the mountain sides were terraced
vineyards. They looked as though some storybook giant
had taken monstrous steps and on each step had
planted grapevines. At the bottom of the hillsides along
the river were little Hansel and Gretel villages like the
ones you see in children's books. I don't know when
I have been as fascinated by scenery as I was during
that first trip of mine down the historic Rhine.

Because it was summer, the boat was crowded
with tourists. They sat all around me on the open deck.
And do you know what a lot of them were doing? They
were playing cards! I was almost as intrigued by the
tourists as I was by the scenery. I swear we could have
sailed out to the North Sea and on to the end of the
world and they would have never known the difference.

I wanted to shout, Wake up! Wake up! A thousand
years of history and legend are gliding past your eyes.

When will you ever see this sort of beauty again? Drink it in now, my friends, because tomorrow may be too late. But I didn't shout, and they continued to play their little game, and the boat moved slowly on.

I have often thought of those "blind" people because through the years I have met too many men and women like them. They are people who fail to see the beauty, color, variety, fascination of life all around them. It doesn't much matter where you and I live, there is always something appealing to see and challenging to do. Here in the United States there are few areas — this is one of the glories of our country — that are not in their own way different, distinctive, intriguing, varient.

I remember lecturing some years ago in a small city in what is commonly regarded as one of the most charming and enticing areas of the United States, and in my opening remarks I said as much. Afterward, a young couple took me to task, rather vehemently, too. They said, "But it's so dull here. There's nothing to see and do. This place is a real drag." And do you know where dullsville was located? In the delightful White Mountains of New Hampshire, a region so redolent of our American past and so entrancing with its human-size mountains and picture postcard scenery that people come from all over the country to revel in and enjoy it.

Many of those visitors would be ecstatically happy to change places with the young couple I talked to. Two people who like blind men and women, or like the tourists on the Rhine steamer, failed to see and enjoy the loveliness shining all about them. For millions of us the pity is not that beauty is missing from our lives; the puzzle is that beauty is here all right, as ubiquitous as earth, air, sunlight, yet, incredibly, we just don't see it.

There is a story, told in several versions, about a company of soldiers isolated in a remote military garrison. Cut off as they were from any outside help, gradually they starved to death. What gives the story its bitter, ironic twist is that the soldiers were there to guard a supply of bags and boxes. It never occurred to them to check the contents. If they had, they would have discovered that the bags were full of grain! Here was food all about them, they were sitting and standing on it, but because they never bothered to investigate what was right under their feet, they starved to death.

That's as cruel a lesson as it is sorry a story. And the moral is this: whatever you do, don't starve to death with bags and bundles of food all about you. Never forget that beauty is everywhere — in things and thoughts, in deeds and dreams, in places and people. For the face of beauty is as endlessly varied as the faces of life and of love. The trick is always to keep one's eyes open, mind alert and imagination flowing free. It's one of the ways, the major ways, we get so much more out of life.

Why Are We So Seldom
at Our Best?

Why are human beings so seldom at their best? Because, to give a summarily simple answer, they so seldom expect the best of themselves. But since a man can't write a book giving only one-sentence answers, and since the answers require a little explication anyhow, let's carry on for a couple of pages.

Elsewhere, we have remarked that people tend to become like whatever they believe in most deeply. Now additionally let us say that people also tend to become like whatever they expect themselves to become like. Take the mournful case of Mr. White, a man who has a low, disparaging opinion of himself, of his attractiveness, abilities and possiblities. Can't we reasonably predict the sort of person he is likely to be? Take, on the other hand, the exemplary instance of his neighbor, Mrs. Brown. She is a woman who has a healthy respect for her own worth, aptitudes and potentialities, and who consistently expects the best of herself. Again, can't we make an equitable judgment without much trouble?

A personality or character quality of Mrs. Brown helps us understand why she so blithely is the way she is. We have described it as "respect for her own worth." We might as easily have said self-confidence and self-image. There is simply no question that people who have a good self-image expect more of themselves — and they usually get it. What we think of ourselves determines our lives more than almost any other factor. It is difficult to believe how much a mental picture can create an actual one. To say that we can think or believe ourselves into superior selfhood sounds like one of those simplistic theories or techniques we sometimes read about in the Sunday supplements.

Yet the ineludible fact is that what we believe is what we tend to become. People can think themselves into depression or they can believe themselves into bliss. The worst and the best are not so much determined by outward circumstance as by inward conviction. Obliquely, William Blake put the matter this way, "If the sun and moon should doubt/they'd immediately go out." Blake may have loved fantasy, but as a way of expressing reality.

The story behind the writing of one of the most influential books in American history tells us something about another way an individual may rise to the peak of her potential. **Uncle Tom's Cabin**, published in 1852, is certainly not notable for its literary qualities. Its significance lies in the fact that it did so much to dramatize (some might say melodramatize) the anti-slavery cause and bring it to a fiery pitch in the decade preceding the Civil War. In any event, it is perhaps our foremost example of anti-slavery literature.

What are of special interest to us, however, are the motives that drove Harriet Beecher Stowe to write her rousing polemic. Mrs. Stowe was the mother of six children. One of them, "the most beautiful and most loved," died, and it was out of that heartrending experience that the inspiration for **Uncle Tom's Cabin**, arose. The bereaved mother wrote, "It was at his dying bed and grave that I learned what a poor slave mother may feel when here child is torn from her . . . There were circumstances about his death of such peculiar bitterness . . . that I felt that I could never be consoled for it unless this crushing of my own heart might enable me to work out some great good for others . . . I have often felt that much that is in **Uncle Tom's Cabin** had its roots in the awful scene and bitter sorrow of that summer."

Mrs. Stowe's book may have been born in the fires of a personal sorrow and suffering, but it was pointed to a high and noble end — the abolition of slavery. In the process of its writing, two revivifying things happened: some of her lacerating anguish lessened and the finest that was in her triumphantly broke through the darkness.

So it was that in her sometimes overwrought fashion, Mrs. Stowe helped America free its slaves. But at the same time, quite unwittingly, she also showed us how to free ourselves from the snare of self-pity and self-concern that the best and bravest within us may shine through.

On Failing to Learn
From Experience

Ever since Henry Flagler and his railroad (and, later, air conditioning) opened up the state as a winter playground, Florida has been America's dream of a South Seas paradise moved 10,000 miles East. For much of this hundred year interval, the Gold Coast, consisting for the most part of Florida's three southeasterly counties, Dade, Broward and Palm Beach, has embodied The Dream.

Palm Beach County, the state's largest, is bounded on its ocean flank by 47 miles of sun-and-sand beaches and azure-and-sapphire waters. It extends from the charming village of Tequesta, includes that premier social resort and island bastion of the rich and famous, Palm Beach, and ends at the tennis clubs and verdurous golf courses of another delightful community, Boca Raton. Palms wave their welcomes everywhere, argosies of yachts dot the sky-blue waters, and the climate is Florida's best because the Gulf Stream swings closer to the peninsula along these sub-tropical shores than it does anywhere else on the Eastern seaboard.

When my wife and I moved to them a dozen years ago, the Palm Beaches seemed (almost) to live up to the Chambers of Commerce's rhapsodic descriptions. But that was nearly a decade and a half ago, which is a long time in Florida. We knew what had happened in Miami and Ft. Lauderdale, but with the innocent faith we Americans have in happy outcomes, somehow we expected our little world would escape the onslaught. When we looked toward Dade and Broward, we saw massive population densities, alarming beach erosion, ever-mounting water shortages, environmental and ecological disasters, traffic frustrations of demonic dimensions, all of them adding up to what seemed like inexcusable shortsightedness.

But — the plague will stop at our borders, we said. People have had time to see what is happening, plan accordingly and learn from experience.

Ah, yes, and good will always triumph and the truth will always out. What we failed to understand is that even we Palm Beachers, splendid, superior creatures though we may be, are still as improvident and myopic as the mere mortals to our south. No, our traffic isn't as congested or our plannnig as chaotic and confused as theirs — yet. But we're moving with dispatch, implacably — in the wrong direction.

What is it about us human beings that we have so much trouble doing what would certainly seem like such an obvious and sensible thing, and that is learn from experience. Wistfully, we dream of an earthy paradise, a utopian wonderland more alluring even, if you can imagine this, than the Palm Beaches. But somehow we seem to end up with the intersection at Indiantown Road and Alternate A-1-A, and if you live in the north part of our county, you know what Dante knew almost 700 years ago.

This has been a playful way of dealing with one of the most discouraging and exasperating characteristics of the human race. But, seriously, think now: That finer, fairer world of which all good souls dream — think how much more likely it might come true if only we could master our history lessons and learn from the experience of others.

Why, the hard way, does each generation have to learn the facts of life all over again? Isn't there some way we oldsters could pass on to our youngsters, more effectively than the race has so far done, a little larger measure of whatever insight, wisdom and truth we have managed to glean? Is it really necessary, is it an immutable law, that every generation has to learn for itself that fire burns when hands are thrust into flame? Is war, which in the past was a foolish and is now becoming a fatal way of resolving differences, to plague us right down to Armageddon?

Regretfully, most scholars and students of human nature will probably answer yes. But it has to be a qualified response. Yes, the child does have to be burned, the heart does have to break, the mistakes do have to be made. Because it is true that failing and falling and fumbling until we learn to walk is the way we have to learn so many of our lessons.

But not all, not all. Surely, if we deserve to be called Homo **sapiens** we ought to be able to do a little better job of gaining from and through the experience of others and so not have to be burned as often, hurt as badly or fooled as frequently as our progenitors were.

To learn much from our own trials and errors, but also to learn an enlightening lot from the experience of others, to realize that profiting from their mistakes is the best kind of profit — if there is any secret to a safer and saner future, we may have it here.

Making the Best of Both Worlds

One of the great explorers of American history was Admiral Richard E. Byrd. He was an outstanding sailor-flier-scholar and a true gentleman. I interviewed him years ago during my brief newspaper career and I still remember thinking what an admirable man he was.

Back in the early decades of this century on his second trip down to the South Pole, Admiral Byrd flew for quite a distance out in the Pacific Ocean along the 180th meridian of longitude. That meridian is the international dateline and of course it's a purely imaginary boundary. When you cross the line, as I have a number of times, you lose a day if you are going West and you gain a day if you are going East.

In writing about his experience, Admiral Byrd said, "All the time we were flying as closely as possible along the 180th meridian. Even without wind drift, for which adequate correction could be made, it is obvious that no navigator could fly along a mathematical line. Consequently, since this was the international dateline, we were zigzagging constantly from today into tomorrow and back again."

For some reason, the Admiral's experience of flying back and forth between two "worlds" or time zones reminds me of another philosopher (which Byrd also was) of a somewhat higher rank. Twenty-five hundred years ago a man who was perhaps the most esteemed of all philosophers, Plato, taught — indeed, this was his basic teaching — that the physical world of things and matter all around us where we live and love and have our being and which we consider to be the real world is not that at all; it is simply a "copy" world. It has only a relative reality. The real world is the world of ideas. Ideas are perfect and eternal. All else is imperfect and transient.

For example, there is one perfect Idea of a palm tree. The palms we Floridians know are simply copies of the idea of a palm as it has impressed itself upon matter. And the copies are always deficient and distorted. They are merely reflections of the "eternal pattern" or of the truth which is the Idea of the palm tree.

So, two worlds: an eternal world of Ideas and Ideals which is real and a physical world in which we dwell which is not real.

All right, a reasonable question: how and why did Plato suddenly materialize out of the mists and end up on the 180th meridian? Because without accepting all his conceptions and convictions and without giving the physical world such short shrift, perhaps we can at least borrow his concept of two worlds, an Ideal one and another which, unlike him, we would call the Real one. And can't we go along with him to this extent and say that (our version of) the real world becomes a little less faulty and flawed as the Ideal is imposed upon it. the Ideal impinging upon the real as we know it and so making it a trace more nearly — ideal.

Now let's borrow Plato's two-world concept and offer our own highly un-Platonic version of it. You and I live in a universe which consists of two worlds: a physical, or so-called real world all about us, and a world of ideas and ideals within us and within history. And superior people are persons who have the ability to "fly" back and forth between the two worlds. What they do is take the ideals, dreams, visions they find in the one world and they cross the meridian and bring them back and put them to work in the other, mundane, what we call real world all around us.

Preachers and philosophers commonly have difficulty interpreting just what it is that the saints and the truly noble souls of the race do or have done. Because, candidly, often they don't seem to have done much of anything. Perhaps the simplest answer is this: by the gentle force of their goodness and wisdom they have moved the ideal and the real a little closer together; they have not only taught us but shown us what the finer, truer, holier is like; the ideal, a murky reality to many of us, is suddenly seen as though the sun radiantly had broken through the clouds.

Down along the 180th meridian Richard E. Byrd flew back and forth between two "worlds." In another mode of flight, we must do the same thing. We must emulate Admiral Byrd's example and fly, not so much from today into tomorrow and back again, but rather from the ideal into the real and back again, and thus combine the best of both worlds.

May your flight plan be flawless, your journey exhilarating and your cargo as priceless as — as wisdom is priceless.

On Walking the
Middle of the Road

Once upon a time there was a man named Master Kung. Today we call him Confucius. He lived in China about 2500 years ago. One of the wisest of men, he promulgated a sane, sensible, down-to-earth philosophy of life that has been perhaps the most influential single factor in Chinese society ever since his day. At the heart of Confucius' philosophy was the conviction that moderation ought to be the governing principle of every person's life. Nothing in extreme, said he; everything in moderation. If life is a road, let us walk the middle of that road and we will most likely come to the goal of peace and serenity we seek. Confucius called it "the middle way."

At approximately the same time, almost 25 centuries ago, there lived another wise man, a Greek this time, named Aristotle. This master of philosophy and metaphysics, inventor of the discipline called logic, father of so much that is fundamental in science, came to much the same conclusion Confucius had reached in far-off China. Only he used the phrase, "the golden mean," to describe his position. The **Nichomachean Ethics**, one of history's truly great books, explores this root problem of moderation and concludes that the goal we should strive for is a reasonable balance of external goods and internal goodness.

Ever since that distant day thoughtful men and women have recognized the universal truth Confucius and Aristotle so lucidly set forth. Marcus Aurelius, wisest of Roman rulers, took this truth to heart and adopted as his motto these words, "Nothing in excess." Apparently whether you call it "the middle way," "the golden mean" or "the law of moderation," what we have in these three simple phrases is one of the most basic and enduring verities of human life.

Here, however, is the problem. One of the little recognized quandries of living in a free society such as ours is that we have so many kinds of freedom — including the freedom to go to extremes, if we want to. Two decades ago during the '60's millions of us wanted to and we went — to an uncharacteristically odd-ball, far-left extreme. Now in the '80's other millions of us have been shifting in an opposite direction and have ended up a far piece right of center.

This leeway we have to veer to extremes is part of the price we pay for freedom, and, be assured, it is worth the price. One hopes, however, that the pendulum will swing back (it always has, so far) and settle for a reassuring stay somewhere near the center. One hopes the German philosopher Hegel was right: that as history shifts from one side to the other, we learn something from both extremes that helps us create a more stable and advanced middle ground.

After all, our current predilection for extremes is not typically American. This nation's history has often been lusty, exuberant and, on occasion, hell-for-leather expansionist, but it has never been really radical or reactionary. Even our revolution over 200 years ago was a remarkably moderate one, led by an avowed conservative, Washington, and probably unpopular with a majority of the people.

What seems to apply to society and history seems equally to apply to the individual. We often speak of people "going off the deep end," which is just one of many ways of saying that they are behaving imprudently, ill-advisedly, extremely. You and I are free, if we choose, to work obsessively, drive too fast, eat and drink too much, shoot drugs, join whatever outlandish movements we care to, and so on almost ad infinitum.

We are free to do whatever we do, but probably we are foolish to do it. Oh, let's be fair about the matter: here's Hegel again — extremes do have their values; we miss a good deal when we always walk the middle of the road; to find new ways and worlds we sometimes have to venture into the wild hinterland where the trails run out. Significant breakthroughs, momentous discoveries are seldom made by the cautious and fainthearted.

But on the whole, prudence, balance, discretion, sound judgment are good words to add to Marcus Aurelius' motto. Over the long haul, the Confuciuses and Aristotles have been right: to get as much as we would like to get from life, we are well advised to treat extremes with care and a fair degree of skepticism, and, generally at least, to follow an ancient precept, Everything in moderation; nothing in excess. Or, in Aristotle's words, "It is clear, therefore, that the mean (or middle) state is what we are to hold to."

On Losing One's Life

Perhaps the most effective of all the many ways of getting more out of one's life is to lose it.

How do you like that for a seemingly nonsensical statement! Yet in the sense it is intended it is one of the sanest, wisest observations you will ever read. Let's complete it and then you will understand it. What we are concerned with here is the sublime conviction that so often we find deeper meaning and satisfaction in life when we lose it, not in death, but in causes, purposes, services larger than our own small selves. This is what Sir Thomas Browne meant in one of the most insightful sentences you are ever likely to read: "To enjoy true happiness, we must travel into a very far country — and even out of ourselves."

On the face of it, this sentiment we are talking about must be difficult to comprehend. To become involved with the headaches and heartaches of others; to take upon one's own shoulders the burdens and miseries of the world — **this**, you say, is the way to get more out of life!

Well, don't charge me with saying it. Charge the saints, the prophets, the holy men and women of the ages. It is they who have understood that to sacrifice one's life in behalf of noble ends is not to lose it, but to find it; to give unstintingly of oneself is to get far more than one gives. The answer to this seeming contradiction is that the ultimate satisfactions of life are not material but spiritual, not self-ish but self-less, and the peace we seek is the peace that comes when we have given our all to the service of the highest that we know.

One thinks of men and women like Gandhi, Schweitzer, Thomas Merton, Jane Addams and Sister Teresa here in our time, and of a heroic procession of martyrs through the ages. Existence is involvement, said Aristotle; it is what we do that justifies our lives. He said it; they lived (and died) it.

Such conclusions sound like religious conviction, and of course they are. But please note that psychology shares them to the full. Both understand that **anomie** may be the most dolorous condition of the human spirit. **Anomie** is a Greek word which can be defined as the desolating sense of meaninglessness and purposelessness that often afflicts displaced people. Another word used to describe much the same condition is alienation which means to feel estranged, unwanted, cut off from. So serious is it that the concept occupies a large space in the lexicon of psychiatry.

This is why both religion and psychology place so much emphasis on whatever is the opposite of **anomie** and alienation, specifically, on the life that has found itself through a sense of meaning, value, purpose and worth. The land of the lost is a fearful place; the land of those who have found themselves, their true selves, is the land we must all be seeking.

And, heaven knows, in a world such as ours one does not have to look very far to find causes and purposes that need his or her help. They are all about us, in our community, country, our crowded, frightened little world. Indeed, the problem is to choose among them and the frustration is that we can help so few. Not a week passes but what with a sense of guilt and something like failure, many of us throw in our wastebaskets pleas for help from all sorts of projects, organizations, movements which we wholeheartedly endorse but simply can't support any more than we presently do.

The primal fact is that human life is an attempt to achieve wholeness and completion. By himself, in the solitude of space, man is a lonely creature wandering naked under the stars. His hunger is for fulfillment. He aches to feel himself at one with his fellows, with the universe, with that ultimate reality we have most often called God. And, let us say it for the third time, he finds what he seeks by transcending his own small self, feeling and becoming an integral part of the larger life around him, and attaining something of that sense of unity and oneness the mystics have always sought. In short, he finds the deepest meaning of his life by losing it.

Perhaps this is why Bertrand Russell, a not notably religious man, ended his book **The Conquest of Happiness** with these words: "The happy man finds himself a citizen of the universe, enjoying freely the spectacle that it affords, untroubled by the thought of death because he feels himself not really separate from those who will come after him. It is in such profound instinctive union with the stream of life that the greatest joy is to be found."

On Having Faith in Life

Faith, as the word is most commonly used, suggests religious conviction. Through the ages, religious faith has supported our race as perhaps nothing else could. There is also, however, something called secular faith, and the two are not necessarily as incompatible as many people suppose.

In Anton Chekov's play **Three Sisters** one of the characters, Masha, says, "I think a human being has got to have some faith, or at least he's got to seek faith. Otherwise his life will be empty, empty . . . How can you live and not know why the cranes fly, why children are born, why the stars shine in the sky. You must either know why you live, or else . . . nothing matters . . . everything's just wild grass." Masha's can be taken either as a statement of religious or of secular faith, or, probably, of both.

It will help us appreciate what is meant by secular faith if we can understand how absolutely essential faith has been, not only to the theologian, but also to the scientist. Science lives by faith. Its history is a story of men acting on faith. Rational, not irrational, to be sure, natural, not supernatural, but faith just the same. Thomas Edison, who was an authority on the subject, said, "We don't know the millionth part of one percent about anything. We don't know what water is. We don't know what light is. We don't know what gravitation is . . . We don't know what heat is. We don't know anything about magnetism. We have a lot of hypotheses about these matters, but that is all. And yet we do not let our ignorance of all these things deprive us of their use."

Since Edison wrote those words, we have made astonishing progress in uncovering and explaining some of the secrets he spoke of. But his point stands firm. There is infinitely more in the universe we don't know than we do know, and there always will be. But the true scientist is a person who believes that behind the unknowable is that which may become knowable, or at least that which is subject to natural law and therefore has rational reason for being.

Erich Fromm once wrote: "The history of science is replete with instances of faith and visions of truth . . . At every step from the conception of rational vision to the formulation of a theory, faith is necessary." He might have gone on to say that along with reason and experimentation, this kind of faith constitutes the foundation of science. Pythagoras, Aristotle and Archimedes; Copernicus, Kepler, Galileo and Newton; Bohr, Oppenheimer and, assuredly, Einstein were, had to be, men of faith. They had to believe in something that was not yet proved, something that at times seemed to defy the accumulated knowledge and wisdom of the centuries. When they flew, one wing was theory, the other was faith. On the Mt. Olympus of science, Albert Einstein is counted among history's half dozen greatest. Yet it was he who wrote these splendid words, "The most beautiful thing we can experience is the mysterious. It is the source of all true art and science . . . To know that what is impenetrable to us really exists . . . is at the center of true religiousness."

What does all such talk about faith and science have to do with you and me? Simply this. The ancient Greeks had a word, **abulia**, which meant the inability to have faith. **Abulia** is a disease of the spirit and it afflicts millions of our contemporaries. Menaced by horrendous deficits, poverty, pollution, over-population, dwindling resources, starvation by whole regions, super power mania, and of course always the Judgment Day Threat of nuclear annihilation, it is little wonder that multitudes have thrown up their hands in despair. We may really have nothing to fear but fear itself, yet that is sufficient to do us in.

Now the antithesis of fear is faith. Faith is the capacity of the human race to believe it can do what it has always succeeded in doing before: overcome obstacles. Or at least enough barriers to let us go by and forward. No intelligent person questions the magnitude of the problems we face, especially the nuclear one. But the answer remains what it has always been: a strong, sustaining faith in the power of the human spirit, not only to survive, but to find solutions and to move ahead from one staging area to another stouter, more secure one. This is not blind faith, it is faith that makes sense, that is vindicated by history, that supported humanity in the past, and that can still lift us up as on wings of eagles and give us the hope and the heart to build the future a little closer to our age-old dream of a kingdom of heaven upon the earth.

What is the Purpose of Life?

If you and I want to get more out of life, it seems reasonable to assume that we are going to have to discover more real point and purpose to this dogged, audacious human adventure that many of our traveling companions apparently find. But when one begins to talk about purpose in life, he is getting into deep philosophical waters. Wise men have struggled with the question for centuries without reaching much common ground. So if I now tilt my lance and charge into the fray, you will have to concede by audacity (even if you have doubts about my perspicacity).

What we are attempting to do here is reminiscent of a short story that was popular in England a century ago. A group of the nation's most notable men were gathered for a country house weekend. After a lengthy loquacious interval, the talk turned to this cardinal question of purpose in life. That took care of the loquacity. Finally one daring soul spoke up and said that life is just a sequence of moments and emotions. Another declared it a solemn mystery. Another, a preface to eternity. Another, a meaningless hiatus between two darknesses. At last, quite unable to reach a consensus, they turned with a sigh of relief to less perplexing matters.

And no wonder. This is one of those primary questions for which we are never likely to find a decisive answer. But that is not to say that there are no answers. Actually, there is quite an assortment, and perhaps the sensible thing for a person to do is to choose what to him is the most intellectually acceptable and emotionally satisfying answer, and proceed to live by it.

Let me be so presumptuous as to suggest an answer that seems to have special appeal to a good many present-day scientists and philosophers. Cut to the bone, it is this: the purpose of life is to grow . . . to become . . . to fulfill itself and its infinite potentialities.

Disappointed? Probably. These few simple words will never unsettle Plato's crown. Yet consider them for a moment. Certainly they are in conformity with everything we know about the world of nature. For if there is any one word that describes nature, evolution, the universe itself, that word is growth. To live is to grow; to fail to grow is to die. The answer, therefore, has a rational justification.

Then it has an emotional appeal. It suggests that by obeying the first law of life, that is, by growing or developing, we can become more mature, advanced, refined creatures than we presently are. (A reassuring thought, certainly, since all of us leave so much room for improvement.) Between birth and death, that potential every one of us has should be perceptively stretched and expanded. We should be a little higher up the hill. This is the most exhilarating of all challenges: to become what we have the potentiality of being.

Finally, our answer has a religious dimension. It suggests that there is an axiological, or value oriented, goal toward which the whole life enterprise is tending. When one looks back over the stupendous course of evolution, he recognizes that during the long haul growth has been persistently upward. It is as though life and the universe itself were struggling to attain an ideal, perfection, the ultimate. Traditionally, religion has called the ultimate God. Scientists use a more technical terminology, but, as Einstein recognized, in their intent they are not far apart.

Now may we not say that the purpose, as it has been from the beginning, is to grow from the imperfect creatures we still presently are to become the unblemished beings we might conceivably be. From dust to glory, from ape to angel is a long, long way, but what a magnificent destiny! — if indeed that it may be.

And here is the most transcendent news of all. So far in its three-or-four-billion year history, life has developed unconsciously, has had no sense that it is part of a fantastic evolutionary process. But recently there has appeared on the scene this astonishing being who is conscious of himself, his past and his future. With the human species, life has suddenly become self-conscious. This means that there is now a creature on the planet who can cooperate with Ultimate Reality, Cosmic Process, Life Force, Ground of Being, God in the supreme task of accelerating the evolutionary pace. More quickly now, we should be able to move from where we are to where ideally we ought to be.

To join with the Ultimate Creative Process ("Some call it evolution, and others call it God") in developing ever-nobler beings and a more nearly sublime world — great starry heavens, could there conceivably be a more exalted life purpose than this!

Parable of a Late Learner

By the side of a great granite rock, a young man stood gazing intently out to sea. As he watched and wondered, another young man, tall, fit, eager for life, walked by. Passing, they waved.

For the tall young man, this was the beginning. He was setting out on a longer journey than ever he dreamed to remote, mysterious lands. He planned to venture far. And indeed he did. As the years fled by and he wandered the world, people would say to him, "What are you seeking?" And he would reply, "I am seeking more from life than I have yet found." "Ah," the people would say.

And so people and places, space and time, a little bit of eternity went by. Always the same query, "What are you seeking?" Always the same reply, "More than I have yet found." Always the same response, "Ah." The road led everywhere, or so it seemed, but never to the goal the seeker sought.

At weary last, as the summers grew shorter, the winters longer, the road harder and the light a little less bright, the tall man came to a strangely familiar place. By the side of a great granite rock, an old man stood gazing intently out to sea. Each recognized the other. Said the one, "Where have you been?" Said the wanderer, "I have been loose in the world, always seeking more from life than I have yet found."

"Ah," said the other man.

"Ah?," said the wanderer. "What do you mean, 'Ah'?"

"I suppose it is a way of expressing surprise. You see, I have spent the passing years here in this dear, familiar place with my friends, my books, my work, and the sea and the world around me, and I have found in life all I have wished to find."

The wanderer was silent. For a long time he spoke no word. Then slowly he said, "I understand." And as the tide ebbed and night came down and darkness fell, he said, "It is true. You are right. I have failed."

"No," said the other. "You have not failed. You have traveled far, seen much, learned more. It is simply, my friend, that you have taken so long to learn what is really so simple, to learn that what you sought so far away is here and now and all about you. But, most especially, that it lies no farther away than your own hands and your own heart."

* * * * * * * * * * * *

Parables are not much in fashion these days, but here's one for you anyhow. A parable is a short allegorical story designed to set forth a moral lesson. It is a disguised way of telling a truth. What you have just read is also a mythic story, in the manner of Ulysses and the Argonauts and King Arthur and his knights and a heroic band of other legendary characters.

And, assuredly, it is an adventure story following in the footsteps of Leif Ericsson and Vasco da Gama and Columbus and Magellan and Raleigh and Drake. And so on, right down to a somewhat less heroic nineteenth century figure, R.H. Conwell and his enormously popular "Acres of Diamonds" lecture (about a man who traveled a lifetime only to find "acres of diamonds" in his own backyard). Always, it seems, this saga of man-in-search-of-himself-and-his-destiny has captured the human imagination.

And well it might. Like the wanderer in our story, perhaps each of us is seeking a Golden Fleece, a "pearl of great price," a marvelous, liberating secret of some sort. Well, our wanderer's end-of-the road discovery may not rank with the revelations of history's immortal myths and legends. Yet in its own simple, down-to-earth way, it stands up well. To learn how to get ever more out of life — things of true value, meaning, import, spirit — is worth the high and heavy price adventurers have often had to pay.

May it be our kindly fate, yours and mine, that we learn the lesson a little sooner, a little more gently . . .

* * * * * * * * * * * *

When Death Comes . . .

All books come to an end. Sometimes, for us readers, regretfully, sometimes relievedly. Likewise life, whether happy or sad, good or bad, eventually comes to an end. Not a very profound statement, perhaps, but, you have to concede, a fundamental one. In all this wide and wonderful world, there is one thing no human being, indeed, no living thing, can escape, and that, or course, is the inevitability of death.

When it comes it leaves those of us who remain behind with a desolating sense of loss, sadness, emptiness, anguish, grief. There is no distress as devastating as that we endure when a loved one dies. And it is a sorrow we should not attempt to conceal or try to suppress. After all, it is hard and real and here, and the wisest thing to do is feel it and let it flow through us so that after awhile it can flow out of us and healing can begin. This walk through the valley of the shadow of death is one march we have to make before we can come out at last on the other side and into the sunlight again.

Incidentally, let me explain that I am not going to talk about this matter of death and deprivation from a religious or theological point of view. There are literally hundreds of different kinds of churches, temples, synagogues and religious groups here in America. Most of them have their own particular beliefs about this matter, as of course they should have, and there is neither space for (nor much prospect of) arriving at a consensus. Perhaps we may simply say that in times of loss and bereavement there is no consolation like that which religion affords.

But there are some additional comforts and assurances that have supported our race through the ages, and a merciful one we have previously talked about is a miracle called memory. By means of this beatific faculty, we can recall our yesterdays, relive our most joyous experiences and bring to life again the friends and loved ones of time gone by. Thus, memory borrows from the past and makes the present and the future brighter and less lonely than they would otherwise be. In fact, memory defeats even death itself by resurrecting so much that was deepest and dearest in our lives. As long as we have our memories, that long we have what has been most precious to us. It is well said, "To live in hearts we leave behind is not to die."

Or consider this assertion: an early Greek philosopher declared that each of us creates his own immortality. We do this by the way we build our own little lives into other lives around us and into the larger world of which we are all a part. Question: did Abraham Lincoln really die in 1865? Answer: not really. Lincoln built himself so inextricably into the life and soul of America that in a sense he is more alive today, or, at least, more influential, than he was over a century ago.

But what about the rest of us who never warrant or achieve Lincoln's kind of acclaim? Haven't we recognized elsewhere that true success is a matter of the quality of character we develop, and the friends we have, and the deeds we do, and the goodness and decency we manifest. Think of all the admirable, enduring things your loved one gave to and got from life, and you will understand what that sage old Greek philosopher meant. We do live on in deeds and achievements, as well as in thoughts and memories.

The voices of experience likewise counsel us to recognize that this grief we feel so keenly is also shared by friends and relatives. When a pain is locked up inside of us and can't escape, it can be as excruciating as a knife in the heart. But when we open ourselves and let that pain out by sharing it with others, it doesn't hurt as much, and in our mutual sorrow there comes a kind of sympathy and solace that is blessedly supportive.

No grief is harder to bear than that which we suffer alone. Friends are a treasure beyond price, and never more so than in the time of our bereavement. They will understand — if we cry, if we say foolish things, but especially if we need someone to hold, or to hold us, against death's coldness. It is not so much what they say — seldom are words less adequate — it is what they are and mean to us that partly fills the void. There is an old reliable remedy for the cure of broken hearts and its names are love and friendship. Your living presence, my dear friend, is as the breath of life to me . . .

Because there are few subjects larger and more mystifying than the one we are considering here, we will have to go on and in our final piece discuss it further. Before we do, though, reflect upon these words of the Spanish writer and philosopher Miguel de Unamuno as they relate to the flame that is friendship: "No, not more light, but more warmth. We die of cold and not of darkness. It is the frost that kills and not the night. "

When Death Comes . . .
and Writes Finis

Since time immemorial human beings have had to make their peace, as best they can, with the inexorable reality of death. Sometimes out of their own tormenting personal experience, wise men and women have written words of such comfort and consolation that untold millions of us have been sustained by them. Needless to say, the Bible has been an incomparable source of sustenance and support. Have any words meant more to bereaved souls than the 23rd Psalm.

Then there are the meditations of sensitive spirits from Socrates and Marcus Aurelius, to Wordsworth and Tennyson, to Dylan Thomas and other contemporaries, and from them we can all learn something and feel much. There is such a lot in life we have to discover the hard way, but perhaps the process can be a little easier if we are receptive enough to listen to what inspired words, pieced together out of their agony by others, can tell us about dying and death and sorrow — and hope again!

One of the lessons they teach us has to do with the relativity of time. When somebody we love dies, we look ahead to the empty spaces and wonder how we can ever face such a forsaken void. But then a curious thing happens. Weeks and months go by, and, as they do, the intensity of our sorrow diminishes and our pain and grief do not hurt as much or as often. Time — blessed time! — is working its ministering magic.

Just as flowers grow over the raw earth of a new-made grave and hide its ugliness with their beauty, so time heals our hurt and brings us compensations we could not have anticipated only a short time before. Somehow mysteriously it transmutes grief into gratitude and despair into new faith and confidence.

When a loved one goes away into what Shakespeare called "the undiscovered country," there is no pain like the one that then overwhelms us. But have you ever realized that pain is the price we pay for loving? If we hadn't loved so much, our sorrow wouldn't be so great and we wouldn't suffer as intensely as we do. Yet who would be so foolish as to say that love is not worth the price we have to pay. Love gives human life its meaning and value as nothing else does. A Roman writer once spoke of "This medicine love that cures all sorrow." He was a knowing man for apparently he understood that after we have worked our way through the dark valley of grief and sorrow, we come out to a place on the other side where the sun is still shining and where love burns more brightly than ever.

In fact, it is even possible to say that death intensifies our love. Now we forget the little faults and failings our loved one had, as do we all, and we tend to remember only what was sweetest and dearest about him or her. Death may destroy bodies, but it does not destroy love. This is why the poets and psalmists have been immortally right when they have sung of the victory of life over death and of love over oblivion.

After all, what is as imperishable as the spirit of a human being, and the memories he bequeathed us, and the influence he had, and the beauty and truth and goodness he built into life, and beyond these even, dearer than all else, the love he left like an eternal flame.

No, there are some things that never die — memory, influence and value, and beauty and bravery and hope, and, forever triumphantly, the wonderwork that we call love. Do not despair, no matter how desolating the dark night of death may seem. For morning **will** come and the sunshine of your love will be as dawn and daylight.

Always remember this:

> That winter is vanquished
> Because spring is victorious;
> That mankind will prevail
> Because love is eternal;
> and that death is defeated
> because life is triumphant!